Green Fables

by:

Anne Buchanan James

Green Fables ©2018

Proper Publishing LLC.
www.properpublishing.info
theproperpublisher@yahoo.com
Exterior & interior design
© 2018 by Proper Publishing LLC.

Agatha illustrations:
Megan Mosier
Georgie Illustration:
Zebo
Magnolia photo credit:
Rita Barnett
Title Credit:
Paul James

Special thanks to the Memphis Botanic Garden and the Memphis Zoo.

Index

Dedication:

Audrey Knight Appleton
1988-2017

Grace, Gabriel, Michael and Oliver
New leaves on a gnarled tree.

Photo courtesy of Rita Barnett

Acknowledgments:

Inspiring Steel Magnolias

Women who exemplify traditional femininity
as well as an uncommon fortitude:

*Rita Barnett, Sally Harper, Susan Lewis,
Juliet DeMarko, Christine Perko Smith,
Carolyn Bishop Kamo, Emily Benoist
Ruffin, Kellie Ann Snyder James,
Dr. Laura Anne James Radel*

To Christopher

Embracing the joy of gardening
and
nurturing a deep love for nature.

Flying Dragon

Agatha had accepted an invitation to visit her dear friend, Magnolia Talbot, Zoo Director in Memphis, Tennessee. The purpose was to identify two trees in the African Lion's exhibit area. Georgie had gained permission from her mother to accompany Agatha on this exciting journey. And Agatha being Agatha, had included Butterbean and Jemima, as well.

At the Zoo, Georgie's pets weren't allowed inside the gates but as the Director was a friend, she permitted the antique automobile with the puppy St Bernard and wise old duck to park in the horticulture area if the animals stayed in the car. Mr. Stevens had promised to keep an eye on the duck and dog. Magnolia Talbot zoomed into the employee parking lot in a Zoo Keeper's cart painted like a bumblebee and scooped up Georgie and Agatha after happy greetings and introductions were exchanged.

Maggie (that's what Agatha called her friend) got right down to business as they drove through the African Veldt where the elephants and rhinoceroses curiously checked out the cart. Next, they entered China were the Panda bears lived.

Georgie tuned out the conversation between the two women and felt as if she were going at warp speed around the world.

Coming to a halt in front of two lionesses and the great lion himself, Magnolia gestured toward two trees loaded with oranges. "We need to have these identified beyond a shadow of a doubt. Visitors are always asking what kind of trees these are." She smiled at Agatha. "I knew you could solve this problem."

Pulling a two-way radio from her pocket Magnolia called the Lion Keeper. The Keeper proceeded to entice the lions into their night house, so they could go into the exhibit area.

Entering the exhibit, Agatha reached up to pluck a 2" diameter orange being careful not to get scratched by one of the wicked looking hook shaped thorns that covered the tree. She handed the fruit to Georgie. "Go ahead and peel it. See what you think."

Working the rind off the pulp, Georgie discovered a lot of seeds and not much fruit. She carefully put the tip of her tongue on the fruit and discovered it to be very, very bitter. Grimacing she glanced at Agatha who smiled. "What you have here, Maggie, are Flying Dragon citrus trees."

"Are they truly citrus trees this far north?" Magnolia stared in wonder at the two trees.

"Yes, these trees can survive temperatures to minus 10 degrees. Poncirus trifoliata, Flying Dragon, is a deciduous tree that can grow 15-20 feet in height. The branches are a corkscrew tangle covered with

2" long thorns. These trees can be grown as a shrub or hedge as a barrier planting acting as a deterrent to dogs, burglars or other unwanted pests."

Georgie grinned. "These are cool! No wonder the lions don't hurt the trees since they are covered in thorns! But the name, Flying Dragon, is super cool! How did they get that name?"

Agatha backed up a couple of steps, hands on hips, staring up at the contorted branches. "I'm trying to remember how they got that remarkable name. I know they came over from China." She paused with a slight frown. "I remember that this was the rootstock shipped to California in 1869, becoming rootstock for commercial seedless naval orange growers of that state. But I simply cannot recall how they came to be called Flying Dragon."

"They are referred to as a trifoliate orange as trifoliate is in reference to what it sounds like — having three leaves. So, a trifoliate orange is simply a variety of orange tree with foliage emerging in groups of three."

Magnolia said, "I knew you could identify these trees, Agatha. Now, we can answer our visitors when they ask. I know they will love the name!" She smiled and turned to go. "Let me treat the two of you to an ice cream at the Cat House Café."

Georgie was totally on board with that idea!

Muddy Shoes

Agatha walked into her friend, Magnolia Talbot's office at the Memphis Zoo. The chair behind the desk was empty. Agatha smiled. The room was still alive with Maggie's personality.

There. In the same familiar spot were a pair of dried muddy shoes. Ready to slip into for inspection of one of the animal exhibits, new construction, crocodile pens, elephant enclosures, horticulture projects, maintenance, one of any of the vast operational needs of the zoo was her friend Maggie's domain. The shoes waited.

Leaning against the edge of the open door, Agatha's mind flashed to her own home. Her mud room always had a pair of dirty rubber boots that never got quite clean when she hosed them off and a dependable pair of sensible brogues caked with soil. Too worn to wear to the grocery but perfect for poking around her garden.

Thinking of her gardening friends, that she knew well enough to be invited into their homes for a cup of tea and some garden talk, she pictured the various old shoes or boots in their different familiar spots.

Turning to leave the office, she nodded to herself. Good old dirty shoes were a friend and necessary item to hardworking folks anywhere in the world.

Tennessee Scuffle

Being the Assistant Director of the Memphis Zoo, Delaney Soxe, kept a constant eye on anything that was out of place. Standing in front of the entrance he studied the large concrete animals that consisted of elephants, rhinoceroses, crocodiles, lions and gorillas, and scratched his head. Something wasn't right. His eyes tracked back and forth. There! Tucked in a shady corner was a bushel basket overflowing with a riot of colored flowers.

Walking over to the half-hidden basket of flowers he breathed in a sweet, lovely fragrance wafting through the air. Knowing the Director's friend, Agatha Chrysanthemum, was visiting he called Magnolia on the radio. "Could you send, Ms. Agatha out to The Avenue, please? I need her help."

Agatha and Maggie walked through the iron entrance gates and found Delaney. He gestured for them to follow.

"Oh! What a heavenly fragrance," said Maggie, as she inhaled deeply.

Agatha bent over the basket inspecting the cut flowers. She tilted her head to the side and frowned, with hands on hips.

"I think we have a message here." She pointed to the bushel basket. "Notice how one side is full of the Passionflower vine and the other side are all Iris flowers. There is a distinct separation of the two." Taking a step back she looked from Maggie to Delaney. "Do either of you know what the Tennessee state flower is?" They both shook their heads no.

"As odd as it is, your state has two State flowers."

Delaney looked at Magnolia and noticed that the look on her face was as blank as what he felt.

Agatha smiled. "Don't worry. Most people haven't a clue what their state flower is but your state, Tennessee, has an interesting history regarding this and that's why it stuck in my mind."

"Back in 1919, the Tennessee senate decided the state could select a state flower. The story begins when some school children named the Passionflower as their favorite. This lasted until 1933. In 1933, claiming the Passionflower was never officially sanctioned by the legislature, the Tennessee General Assembly designated the Iris as the Tennessee state flower. This was not accepted by the Passionflower folks. A scuffling ensued between Passionflower supporters and Iris champions. The arguments between the two crusaders were spirited and intense. It took many years, before a happy medium was found. The Passionflower was renamed the state's official *wild*flower and the Iris was renamed as the state's official *cultivated* flower."

Maggie smiled. "That explains why I've seen the Iris flower on our license plates."

Agatha nodded in agreement.

The two women looked at Delaney as he began humming. Then he threw back his head and in a beautiful deep base began singing.

When it's Iris time down in Tennessee
I'll be coming home to stay
Where the mockingbird sings at the break of day
A lilting love song gay
Where the iris grows where the Harpeth flows
That is where I long to be
There's a picture there that lives in memory
When it's Iris time in Tennessee.

"Why that was just wonderful, Mr. Soxe!" Agatha grinned and clapped her hands. "You have a beautiful voice!"

Delaney lowered his head and shook it back and forth, as a broad smile slid across his face. "Aw, shucks, Ms. Agatha. I do enjoy a good song! And I'm pretty sure that's our state song!"

Maggie gave him a mock salute and said, "Well done Delaney! I wouldn't be able to name our state song to save my life!"

Bending over the bushel basket, Agatha continued ruminating on the history of the two flowers. "The passionflower is more commonly known as the maypop. They grow wild in all the southern states. We have them all over the place in Florida. Ocoee is the Indian name for them. You have the Ocoee river here in Tennessee and we have a city named Ocoee in

Florida. Native Americans thought the ocoee was the most beautiful of flowers."

"Are Iris an easy flower to grow?" Delaney asked. "My grandmother had them everywhere."

"Very. These perennials are very hardy, growing from potato-like roots called rhizomes. There is a huge variety of color with the most common color being a purply blue.'

'By the way," Magnolia looked around the avenue, "Where are Georgie and gang?"

Agatha took off her straw hat wiping her brow. "They are getting some exercise playing frisbee. Butterbean and Jemima outdo each other racing to catch it." She smiled. "I think they needed some vigorous activity after our visit to the Memphis botanical gardens earlier. They have several hundred types of Bearded Iris on display there. Is just beautiful. Placing her hat back on her head, she said, "Speaking of which, I need to go gather them."

"Is this mystery solved to your satisfaction, Delaney?" Maggie asked.

"Yes, Ms. Maggie. Your friend, Ms. Agatha is one special gardener. I'd call on her anytime!"

The Satsuma Mandarin

Agatha Chrysanthemum was bent over poking around in her garden when a young girl with crooked pigtails burst through her garden gate. Jerking upright, she said, "Heavens to Betsy, Georgie, what in tarnation is your hurry?"

"Oh, Agatha, quick! There's a fight. Jimmy and Phil are yelling about Phil's tangerines going missing. Phil says Jimmy stole them!"

Agatha frowned as she placed a gnarled, arthritic hand on the small of her back. "Well, it is October, and I noticed that Phil's Satsuma trees were full of fruit. Now, through December is when the mandarins mature." She glances at Georgie who was fidgeting. Both hands were worrying her frayed bibbed overall front pockets. "The word mandarin is the preferred name over tangerine. You did ask me to teach you the proper names of plants."

Georgie nodded biting her lower lip in impatience. She wanted to get back before her friend Jimmy Longknife was decked by the huge, middle-aged Phil.

Jimmy lived in the Choctaw swamp and was an easy target for Fast Phil, as Georgie liked to call the money-loving man.

Agatha said, "C'mon then. We best be going. I assume you rode Peaches over here?"

Georgie grinned. "'Course I did. She's behavin' like a champ today!"

Peaches was an old motorcycle with a sidecar whose color had faded to something between yellow and orange. Georgie's ride around the Perdido Key community. A village on the north coast of the Gulf of Mexico. Being just twelve years old, she didn't have a driver's license, but the many sandy roads have her freedom to roam and explore.

Agatha pulled a scarf from around her neck over her star hat and tied it in a bow under her chin. Rubbing the dirt off her hands, she trotted out the gate to the dilapidated contraption. She squeezed herself into the sidecar and smiled at Georgie giving a nod.

The girl jumped onto the bike like mounting the back of a horse, and in one fluid motion, her right leg pushed down on the kick starter. Peaches gave a belch, hiccupped, and lurched into forward motion. Peaches top speed was somewhere between a trotting horse and a hopping rabbit depending on how much gas got through the fuel line.

As they rounded the corner onto Magnolia Lane a grove of trees filled with brilliant reddish orange, tender, and ripe Satsuma Mandarins filled their view. Under these trees was a giant of a man at six feet six inches bent over holding fourteen-year-old Jimmy by the shoulders as he yelled at him.

Peaches hadn't even stopped before Agatha, clambered over the edge and zoomed like an enraged hen to the man and boy.

"Stop, this instant, Phil Wiggins! Have you even given the boy a chance to talk?" She glared up at the giant wagging her finger. Phil let go of the boy and took a deep breath, shaking his head.

Agatha motioned for Jimmy to join Georgie then she took Phil's strong arm and led him away from the children as she said, "Tell me about these trees, Phil. Tell me why you planted all the citrus trees in this northern part of Florida?"

As Phil tried to glance back at the kids, Agatha firmly propelled him forward. "Talk." He took another deep breath and let it out in a big gust of air. "I needed a supplemental income to my retirement. After researching what I could grow on these ten acres, I decided on Satsuma tangerines."

"Mandarins." Agatha corrected him quietly.

"Yes, Satsuma Mandarins are a crop that need cool winters and hot summers. Exactly what we have here in the panhandle of Florida."

"Are they native to this area?" Agatha asked even though she knew good and well, that they weren't. In fact, she probably knew their history better than Phil, but she got him talking.

"Satsumas probably started in China, but they were first reported in Japan more than 700 years ago, where it's their main citrus crop now. The wife of the U.S. minister to Japan sent these trees from Satsuma, the name of the Japanese province in 1878. She gets credit for their name. During 1908-1911, approximately a million 'Owari' Satsuma trees were imported from Japan and planted through the lower Gulf Coast states from the northern Florida Gulf coast to Texas, where a huge tangerine industry developed. But many freezes over the years killed the trees. But it is still the biggest commercial citrus grown in the southern parts of the states bordering the northern Gulf of Mexico."

He stopped and turned his head to look down at the gentile, elderly woman under an enormous scarf and hat. "You did that to me on purpose."

Agatha released his arm and reached for one of the succulent Mandarins hanging just over her head, plucking it off the branch. She began to peel the loose rind from the orange, flattened sphere as she stared down the row of trees marching through the orchard. "Don't you think you need to cool off a little?" She turned her searching blue eyes on him. "What makes you think Jimmy Longknife stole your oranges?"

Phil had the grace to look chagrined. "Because he was there."

Agatha continued staring not saying a word.

"I guess I need to apologize to the boy." He shuffled his feet, and his tone turned a little harsh. "He is that loafer, swamp-dwelling, Jimmy Longknife's son though."

"Do you mean the highly skilled tracker and able to live off the grid, Choctaw Indian, who is more intelligent than all this neighborhood combined? That Jimmy Longknife? Really, Phil? You wish to accuse his son? Do you have any proof?" Her words came like marksman bullets to the large man's ears.

"He was eating one."

"Just like I am?" She stared at him as she ate each little section one by one. "Let's go find those children, so you can say you're sorry."

Love bugs in Florida

Agatha stomped on the break of the butter yellow 1937 Cord 812 Supercharged Phaeton convertible which caused her large straw hat to topple forward. Totally flustered, as she never did anything abruptly in this automobile. She'd just seen a love bug, and they had no business flying around at this hour after she purposefully left the house at 6:00 AM to avoid the horrid little flies also, known as March flies. Being closely related to mosquitoes and gnats didn't endear them to her in the least.

She pushed back the hat, having a think. Just like Winnie the Pooh.

Love bugs descended like a plague on the southern part of the country during the spring month of April-May and autumn month of August-September. She rarely drove her three prized antique automobiles during these months as they were her retirement investment and she didn't want the cars paint finish damaged due to smashed love bugs. Some people spread baby oil over the vehicles hoods in hopes of aiding the removal of the squashed bugs. She wasn't about to do that to her treasures.

She concluded her think and backed out of the two-car garage. Motoring on down Magnolia Lane, she slammed on the brakes again. "'Pon my soul, this is a morning! I'm so very sorry Butters (that is what she called this particular car), but there is a box in the road worry box is not supposed to be!" She pondered the situation a few more moments then opened the door which swung front to back, unlike modern car doors which opened back to front.

As she walked to the box which had a raggedy, faded beach towel draped over the top, she heard faint mewing sounds. Lifting a corner of the tower she saw four baby chicks. "Oh, my. You're not kittens at 'all. You're chickens!"

At that moment, a rattling bark announced the arrival of Georgie on Peaches. A dilapidated old motorcycle with a sidecar.

"What ya' doin, Agatha? What's in the box?"

Hands on hips, Agatha said, "Baby chicks! Four baby chicks to be precise. Poor little orphans. Guess somebody had one too many eggs hatch out." She glanced around the quiet neighborhood. "I didn't know anybody near me even had chickens." She grinned at Georgie. "Do you think they eat love bugs?"

Georgie grinned back. "You told me nothing ate those horrible love bugs! Although you did say, some studies have shown that they'd be found in the gizzards of robins in quails." She tilted her head with crooked pigtails swinging. "I remember you said fungi is about the only thing that is a true natural predator of love bugs. It affects the larvae or something like that."

"My stars! You do remember, Georgie! More research is needed on the larvae idea, but they do know that nine different species of fungi affect love bug larvae. Well done, Georgie." she being at the girl sitting on the bike then turned her attention to the box at her feet.

"What shall we do with these baby chicks?" Georgie said, "Well since it's Saturday we could take them to the lady at the farmers market on Palafox Street. She told Mom that she could never have too many chickens." Georgie was hoping Agatha would invite her to ride in the gorgeous mile-long Butters. "We could put her to the test and see if she means it?"

Agatha considered the idea. "Your mother get called to work today?"

Georgie's mom was a home health care nurse and her hours were long and unpredictable.

"Yup! Just for a few hours this morning."

"Want to ride with me to the market?"

Georgie bounced up and down on Peaches seat. "Oh, yes! Can I park or in your driveway?"

Agatha nodded yes and picked up the box, carefully placing it on the floor of the passenger seat.

After parking peaches in the shade of a giant live oak tree, Georgie carefully settled herself in the passenger seat with legs on either side of the box.

Butters purred serenely down Gulf Beach highway.

Georgine knew that the car was content to be out on the road on a beautiful name morning. Dipping her right hand up and down in the air current like a plane flying beside the car, she asked, "Do love bugs ever do anything besides mate? And where do they come from?"

"Usually the females remain on or close to the ground, with males swarming about one to five feet off the ground. The swarm can get as high as 20 feet with up to forty males in it. Males hover over the females orienting themselves to the wind to make copulating easier. They live just long enough to mate, feed, disperse and deposit a batch of eggs. About three to four days. And yes, that's about all they do. Hence the name, love bugs."

"Ugh," said Georgie. "That's horrible." Agatha had both wheels on the large steering wheel as she glanced at Georgie.

"There are two known species of love bugs in the U.S. One is a native species, and the other is an invasive species that first appeared in Louisiana in the 1920s. They spread through Mississippi, Alabama and reached us here in Florida in 1947. Now they've migrated up through Georgia and South Carolina. For some infernal reason, they are often found near highways and are a huge problem for all vehicles. Clogging radiators, getting into Refrigeration equipment on trucks, making windshields slimy. Just an all-around nuisance!"

Georgie nodded. "I pulled Peaches into Carson's Country Store to gas her up and was going to wash her headlight, but the bucket of water was so stinky with love bug slime and guts that it was awful!"

Agatha grimaced. "We are going to skedaddle to the market then get Butters back home in the garage before 9 a.m. Now buckle up, young lady!"

A pest insect is merely a bug where you don't want it

Mag Gott and Arthur Pod were sitting on the porch ruminating on the importance of insects. They both favored chemical-free gardens, which wasn't always possible they reflected solemnly.

"I was speaking to Agatha, yesterday, about the insects in her garden," mused Mag. "She told me she had plenty of wildlife in her garden, so she didn't suffer from too many insects, as they get eaten. She has worms, toads, frogs, and bats, and mentioned that birds helpful, too. Wrens, finches and even a woodpecker or two. She said she has even seen a fox wander through, probably looking for one of her Cochin Bantam chickens!"

Arthur crossed his legs, "An insect, specifically a pest insect, is merely a bug where you don't want it. Such as those dreadful Japanese beetles that are swarming on my grapes and peaches! I sprayed my roses last year, but I am just picking off the beetles as I see them (handfuls of them) rather than waging an all-out war on them this year."

"I tried using a Pheromone trap. I put it 50 feet from my roses and it helped." Mag said, swatting at a fly.

"Weather is an important factor in pest insect population size, too," continued Arthur. "For example, during hot, dry, summer weather, mosquito populations usually decline. During cool, wet, spring conditions, some insect populations are reduced – fungal disease may attack and kill vulnerable insects and eggs. I look at insect pests as consumers. They take something away from humans. Take the Columbine leaf miner. It lays eggs on the underside of columbine and aster leaves. The maggot makes winding tunnels in the leaf, feeding between the upper and lower epidermis, overwintering in the soil. I don't control them. They make my flowers look hideous! What gets my goat is something like the Apple Maggot or railroad worm, burrowing through apples, leaving brown trails and I control those with fruit tree spray."

"I don't like the way flies are biting this year," Mag griped, swatting at the nagging pest overhead, again. "They are especially annoying when I try and garden."

They both realized that they were being exceedingly pessimistic.

"Arthur, if anyone listened to our conversation they would wonder why we bother at all!"

Arthur smiled and said, "Since the Garden of Eden we have had the good and the bad or as Clint Eastwood would say, *The Good, The Bad and The Ugly*!"

Agatha offers tips on caring for fruit trees

Wabash River Drive
S.E. Illinois, Indiana Border

Dear Agatha,

My husband and I recently bought 25 acres and an old home on the banks of the Wabash River.

There are a few old apple trees on a high bluff overlooking the river and a small orchard on some low ground. We would like to add some fruit trees but don't know which varieties do best in this area. We would appreciate it so much if you could help us. Also, should we add to one of these locations or organize the new trees to create one large orchard?

I promise I'll make a pie for you out of Jonathan apples, which I know are your favorite.

Thank you,
Ura Peach

Dear Ura,

What a charming place you must have and how delightful to have a home orchard! Growing fruit trees can be such a soothing and satisfying hobby for home gardeners.

Fruit trees differ considerably in the amount of care required because of the severity of insect and disease attacks. And the length of time from bloom to harvest can vary drastically among types and varieties of fruits.

Fruit trees prefer an easily worked, deep and well-drained soil with a sub-soil that permits deep rooting. Fruit bearing trees dislike 'wet feet' caused by wet soils with poor water drainage. Cherries, peaches, nectarines, and apricots are especially sensitive.

The fact that you have an orchard on both high and low ground is significant. Spring frosts and winter cold are both hazards to fruit crops in this area. Cold air, being heavier than warm air, will flow to lower areas and warm air will rise to higher areas when the wind is not blowing. Therefore, high elevations should be selected for fruit plantings, especially in rural areas. Ura, that high bluff is a great area.

Resistance to damage by cold temperature varies among types of fruits and knowing the ratings for fruit trees can be helpful.

Rating: Most sensitive -- apricots, sweet cherries. Most sensitive -- peaches, nectarines, Japanese-type plums. Moderately sensitive -- pears, sour cherries, European-type plums. Least sensitive -- apples.

In rural areas, like yours, fruit trees need protection from spring and summer prevailing winds. In this area, these winds are southwesterly, so windbreaks should be located on the south and west sides of the fruit planting. Protection from northern winds during the winter is not needed. Windbreaks protect an area on the downwind side five times as far as the height of the windbreak. Also, of course, lots and lots of sunshine. Fruit trees do best in full sun. They can tolerate partial shade, but the quality of the fruit produced will be lower.

Therefore, the soil, elevation, air drainage, windbreaks, and sunshine are all critical for a thriving home orchard. I suggest not planting any fruit trees in your low area. Not even the least sensitive fruit in this area, which is the Golden Delicious Apple.
I look forward to one of your fabulous Jonathan apple pies.
Happy fruit growing.
Always,
Agatha

Agatha talks about unwanted guests in vegetable gardens

After shivering her way through the frozen food section of an enormous supermarket, Agatha pushed her grocery cart into the slightly less frigid air of the produce department. She stopped next to a woman who was picking up round cabbages and putting them back down. Exchanging smiles, "Why is it, year after year, my cabbages suffer from worms, and I still have a compulsion to plant the same three rows every spring?"

"We are 'creatures of habit' when it comes to our vegetable gardens," Agatha ruminated. "Certain related crops are susceptible to the same problems. There are Cole crops (cabbage family), Cucurbits (cucumber family), and Solanaceous (tomato and potato family). If possible, you should avoid planting any of the vegetables within these groups in the same location more than one year. For example, cabbage and turnips should not be planted in the same location for two succeeding years. Included in the cabbage family are broccoli, brussel sprouts, cauliflower, kohlrabi, rutabaga, and turnips. It is important to rotate the vegetables in the garden to different locations every year."

The woman took a better look at Agatha, "That is very interesting. You seem to know quite a lot about vegetables."

"Oh no," Agatha shrugged, "I know very little, and the more I learn, the more I find I don't know. I can tell you that cabbages are a good source of vitamins and they thrive during the spring and fall seasons. In the spring, once the cabbages have finished, they should be pulled up and followed by planting late beans, cucumbers, or corn. By rotating your location of the vegetables in your garden every year, you will be doing something to help control the garden pests such as cabbage worms. There are three species of cabbage worms (imported cabbage worms, cabbage loopers, and diamondback worms). All of these are commonly found in this area and attack the head and the leaves of cabbage and related Cole crops. Imported cabbage worms are velvety green caterpillars. The moth is white and is usually seen during the day hovering over plants in the garden. That signals the start of an infection. Cabbage loopers ("measuring worms") are smooth, light-green caterpillars. The cabbage looper crawls by doubling up (to form a loop) and then moving the front of its body forward. The moth is brown and is active at night. Diamondback worms are small, pale green caterpillars that are pointed on both ends. The moth is gray, with diamond-shaped markings when the wings are closed. Cabbage worms are quite destructive and will ruin the crop if not controlled. They are even worse in fall planting than in spring gardens."

"How do I protect my cabbages from these awful worms?" asked the woman.

"You need to use a chemical insecticide from the time they are transplanted into the garden until harvest," replied Agatha. "It is almost impossible to raise Cole crops in this area without controlling these pests. You need an insecticide that has the common name of permethrin in it. There are several trade names. Ask your garden center or read the label and follow the directions faithfully. Be sure and wash the cabbages before eating."

"Thank you for helping me," said the woman. "I love that I will now always have a fond memory of this visit to the cabbage section of the produce department," she said. "By the way, my name is Belle Pepper."

"And I am Agatha Chrysanthemum."

All about roses and "Rose Rustlers"

Agatha was bent over poking around in her garden when her newly married neighbor, Marion Haste, came bustling through her gate and asked her in a breathless voice if she had ever heard of a group of people called "Rustlers. Not cow rustlers, but "Rose Rustlers." A group of 15 people had just knocked on her door and asked if they could examine her rose bush that they had seen in the corner of her garden and could they have some pieces to root? "Who are these people, Agatha?" asked Marion. "And what is a Rose Rustler?"

"Not to worry, Marion," said Agatha, "Let me explain. Rose rustlers are a group of people who are interested in collecting and growing old roses, or antique roses. There are four types of roses that most people are familiar with: Hybrid Teas, Floribundas, Grandifloras, and Climbers. It was near the turn of the century that the popularity of one class, the Hybrid Teas, with their classic bud form and striking color, swept almost every other type of rose off the market. The Hybrid Tea is the long-stemmed rose you buy at the florist. A Floribunda has smaller blooms, and the blooms are often in clusters. Flowers may be single, semi-double, or double. A Grandiflora is a prolific bloomer from spring until frost. Flowers are usually clustered but may be separate. Also, they are generally larger plants."

"The group of people in your yard are interested in collecting and identifying old or antique roses. The American Rose Society classes any rose introduced before 1867 as 'old', but most collectors are more lenient, considering any rose 75 years old, or more, as eligible. One telltale sign is the unforgettable true rose perfume that is in undiluted form in most old roses. The fragrance is not as rich and diversified in the majority of modern roses. Older roses are riding an immense wave of popularity right now," Agatha explained while wiping her hands. "Unlike inanimate heirlooms preserved among families, old roses are a living reminder of our heritage. The colors, the perfumes and their vigor and grace help keep the past alive. The flowers are not copies or 'restored.' They survived before pesticides, sprinklers or other modern gardening practices. That's why we can find them in cemeteries and old homesite. Sometimes centuries later."

"The majority of old roses came from the Orient and Europe. China and Tea roses are from the Far East and are the oldest. Some in China can be dated back to 1,500 years ago. In Europe, these China and Tea roses were crossed with Gallicas, Musks, Centifolias, and Damasks, which gave rise to a new class of garden roses: the Noisettes, Bourbons, Portlands, Hybrid Perpetuals, Polyantha, and

Grandifloras. There have always been a few rosarians who preferred the older varieties. A movement started in the 1930s to preserve old garden roses. Interest in old roses is increasing today."

"The group you have in your garden, Marion, is an organization of people dedicated to collecting and grouping old roses," Agatha said. "Collectors never remove plants, they only take cuttings---a very inexpensive pursuit, and interesting too. Come on, Marion, let's go talk to them and see if they can identify your rose. I already know that the shrub you have is a 'Souvenir de la Malmaison,' a Bourbon rose introduced in 1834. Let's see if they get it right."

Amaryllis bulbs can brighten winter days

The grim days of January and February loomed ahead. Emma Rillis had a double motivation to fill her eastern bay window full of colorful plants. The challenge was to get plants that could be encouraged to bloom and provide color in the winter rather than their normal Spring or summer season. She, not only, wished to enliven the gray days of winter, she had also, entered a photography contest, and hoped to capture the different stages of bulb growing.

Emma loved gardening, but her busy schedule allowed her little time to indulge in this passion. She needed information. She invited Agatha Chrysanthemum for tea. Settling themselves in comfortable wing chairs, Agatha was delighted to share her knowledge and make suggestions to Emma as they sipped their tea from delicate bone china cups.

"The definition of a bulb is any plant that stores its complete life cycle in an underground storage structure." As she relaxed and enjoyed the soothing warmth from the tea, Agatha continued, "When we force bulbs to bloom indoors in the Winter, it is an artificial process, and truthfully, the bulbs get pretty exhausted and are quite unfit for similar use again. If they are planted in the Spring among shrubs or in odd corners of the garden, they are usually capable of a little cheerful bloom in the following years. If you were going to force some bulbs, September is the right time to start, and that type of cultivation is a whole other 'kettle of fish' that needs at the minimum six weeks to be successful. What I envision for you, Emma is an African native bulb called Amaryllis. They have a magnificent bloom, and you can get some amazingly brilliant colors."

"I once saw a mass planting of Amaryllis in the tiny town of Yemassee, South Carolina. It was a magnificent display and such a delight to see them growing outside, which is possible in regions with mild winters."

Agatha sat up. "You can skip the forcing process and purchase bulbs, right now, that come in a kit that includes a pot and some fiber that you plant it in. I suggest having at least 2/3 of the bulb above the surface, and the Amaryllis bulb likes to be crowded in the pot. A six-inch pot will easily accommodate a large bulb. The bulbs are huge and contain a tremendous amount of food inside. Consequently, success is quite sure when growing this bulb indoors."

"I am familiar with the different stages of the Amaryllis," responded a delighted Emma. "They will make wonderful photographs. I can picture the first peek of the leaves out of the top of the bulb, the long stalk with a bulging top, the top of the stalk breaking open slowly as the blossoms burst out. Oh, Agatha, it's perfect."

"There is a variety called Bella Donna that I grew once," remembered Agatha, wistfully. "I don't see it very often anymore. It has a pink tone and is often referred to as the 'naked lady' because the flowers appear alone, the leaves are produced later on."

They set their teacups down and smiled with the satisfaction of having arrived at an agreeable and beautiful solution.

Asian Longhorned Beetle extremely destructive to healthy hardwood trees

Agatha was reading the Chicago Tribune while the rain beat steadily against the windowpanes. It made a lulling, comforting sound that pulled her eyelids slowly downward and then her eyes stopped on an article that caught her attention and they snapped wide open. This is what it said:

Asian Longhorned Beetle Alert Found in Chicago.

An infestation of the Asian longhorned beetle (Anoplophora glabripennis) was discovered in July 1998 in the city of Chicago. This tree-damaging beetle has a history of interceptions in solid wood crating materials originating from Asia, but the only other known infestations in the United States are on Long Island, New York. Within days of its detection in the tree-lined Ravenswood neighborhood of Chicago, city, state, and federal officials developed tactical plans to prevent the spread of and eventually eradicate this potentially devastating pest.

Asian longhorned beetles are native to China, Korea, and Japan. Adult beetles are large, conspicuous insects, an inch to an inch and a quarter long with prominent antennae ("long horns") stretching to twice the body length. In China, it is commonly referred to as the "starry sky beetle" because of 40 or so white dots marking its shiny, coal black body. Equally notable are the alternating black and white bands of the elongate antennae.

This beetle is extremely destructive to many species of healthy hardwood trees. Maples (including Norway, sugar, silver, and red), boxelder, poplar, willow elm, mulberry, black locust, horse chestnut, black pear, and plum are all reported hosts. Extremely high attack densities or repeated attacks over a period of years ultimately will result in the death of the tree. Because of this beetle's extensive host range, its preference for healthy, living trees, and its suspected ability to survive throughout North America, it is considered a major economic threat to the landscape and hardwood forests of this state and nation. Other than the presence of the beetle itself, homeowners should be aware of several symptoms in trees that may point in a possible infestation:

- Large, circular holes ⅜ to ½ inch in diameter in the trunk or main branches
- Heavy accumulations of coarse sawdust in branch crotches or at tree bases
- Heavy sap flow from holes in bark
- Mid-summer leaf yellowing and leaf drop

Any tree, particularly a maple, willows, or poplar, that exhibits a combination of these symptoms should be brought to the attention of the experts.

Agatha put down the paper and went outside in the rain to do a close check on her maple trees. After examining them carefully, she breathed a deep sigh of relief as none of them had any of the symptoms. "Whatever, next," she thought. "Beetles from crate material from Asia that can wipe out all the maple trees in this country!" I pray it never spreads.

Bean salad sparks table talk

"Not much can compete with the fragrant freshness of peas and beans straight from the vegetable garden. Beans can be planted at two-week intervals from early May until early August. That way you will make sure you will have a continuous crop throughout the summer."

Agatha was talking to two of her friends that had taken her for a surprise lunch at the Ritz in St. Louis, Minnie Van Ryder and Belle Pepper. The food was exquisite, and the atmosphere was lovely.

"Minnie, did you know that the bean plant, which is a tender, warm season vegetable, ranks second in popularity to the tomato in Illinois gardens?" Agatha asked.

"No, I didn't, but if this bean salad is an example, I understand why!" Minnie replied while spearing beans with her fork.

"What did you order?" inquired Belle, as she looked at the delicious arrangement on Minnie's plate.

"It is called 'Warm Runner Bean, Walnut and Bacon Salad. These walnuts are toasted to bring out the flavor and I think they have put a touch of water in the vinaigrette to delay the vinegar hitting the palate--that rather sharp sensation when you first taste a salad," delicately shuddered Minnie.

"This is perfection," she sighed.

Agatha and Belle both leaned toward Minnie's plate and peered at it with interest. Each longed to poke at the salad with her fork to try to figure out exactly what was in it.

"Do you think you can figure out the recipe?" Belle asked quietly.

"Well, I know there is bacon and after browning it, I'm guessing they toasted it with walnuts for 5-10 minutes to bring out the flavor. I think the dressing is balsamic vinegar, a touch of mustard and more walnuts. They must have tossed this with green runner beans and viola! There you have it!" Minnie laughed.

"The English call it a 'runner bean.' We Americans call it green bush or green pole," Agatha said.

"You can see how crisp the beans are in your salad Minnie, and that means they are fresh, of course, but they have also been picked when the pods are firm and crisp and before the seed in the pod has developed significantly. Beans should be picked after the dew is off the plants and they are thoroughly dry. Picking wet beans spreads bean bacterial blight, a disease that will seriously damage plants. Be careful not to break the stems or branches. The bean will continue to form new flowers and produce more beans if all pods are removed before the seed matures.

"The most common problems are bean mosaic disease, bacterial bean blight and the beetles that feed on the bean plants. The mosaic disease and bacterial bean blight can be controlled by planting disease resistant varieties. The beetles are controlled by an insecticide."

Satisfied with a delicious lunch, Belle and Minnie paid the bill and Agatha thanked them for a wonderful surprise lunch at the Ritz, saying, "Food should have a dash of surprise, like your bean salad, Minnie, and charm, to be truly memorable--just like lunch at the Ritz."

Brazilian Adventure

It was oven-hot in the attic, as Agatha searched for the well-seasoned old suitcases that had been inherited from her parents. Good, hard leather with solid brass latches. Her parents had traveled the world before WWII and now, Agatha was taking a short trip to Brazil, South America. She was hoping to fit a good stout, collapsible 'walking stick' in her luggage, too.

Her newly married neighbor, Marion Haste, was going to take care of her plants while she was away.

Marion came over so Agatha could show her which plants to water and any other etc.'s that might need to be done.

"Agatha, what language do they speak in Brazil? Do you think you need to take a gun for snakes?" asked Marion nervously.

Agatha was very hot from the attic and was trying to convince a stubborn 'walking stick' that it certainly could fit into one of the large suitcases.

"They speak Portuguese in Brazil, Marion and no, it isn't necessary for me to tote a gun along. My 'walking' stick will suffice for any contingency that might arise. Brazil is a beautiful contrast of wilderness and sophistication," continued Agatha. "This country covers almost half of South America. The coastline of Brazil has over 11,919 miles of white sandy beaches. Brazil also, borders all the nations of South America with the exception of Chile and Ecuador. I read an interesting statistic Marion, which makes me realize I am going to be an exception. Over 70 percent of the 160 million inhabitants of Brazil are under 30 years old."

"Heavens, Agatha!" exclaimed Marion; "You will stand out."

"They have the Amazon Forest, Ignacu Waterfalls, some of the most famous beaches in the world and very sophisticated large cities. Just to name a few of the impressive wonders of that country."

"What is your main reason for going?" asked Marion.

"September is spring there and that is when the country is literally awash with flowers. There is a fair going on called Expo flora in a place called Holambra. A place full of Dutch people. That is a wonderful and compelling reason for going. However, the main reason is to spend time with my dear friend, Idda Costa Littleless. We will visit her two farms and meet all of her relatives. I also hope to do a little shopping, since our dollar is worth more there. Their currency is called a Real (R$). Things in general will cost a little less."

"Now remember, Marion, my maidenhair fern needs the soil to be kept moist. Don't worry about watering the grass. Keep my Rudbeckias watered, their color enlivens late summer. My blue and purple Michaelmas daisies need water, too. Please, help yourself to all the Red Delicious apples you can use. Enjoy the September display of one of my favorite plants, the Japanese anemone. Their flowers are always such a pleasure in autumn, continuing as they do so late into the season. My favorite are white Anemone x hybrida 'Honorine Jobert' and pink Anemone hupehensis 'September Charm'."

"Don't worry about a thing, Agatha. I will love it all as if it were my own," assured Marion.

"And Agatha?"

"Yes, dear?"

"Don't forget to take a straw hat."

"Of course not, dear. I wouldn't leave without one."

Brazil offered beautiful flowers

The phone was ringing. Agatha sighed as she stopped sweeping the leaves off of the porch. Everything was dry. Several hours of a nice gentle rain would give everything a good drink, she thought as she reached for the phone.

"Agatha! This is Ginger. Ginger Wild. Welcome home from Brazil! I want to know all the details. How was it?"

"Oh Ginger! It was all so wonderful that it is hard to describe it in a few words. I would need a week of talking but let me put my feet up and I will highlight a few of my experiences. It was very, very dry there. It is Spring but, in some places, it hasn't rained for 100 days, so there weren't as many flowers blooming as normal, but in my opinion, there were still plenty of flowers."

"Did you make it to the flower expo in the Dutch town of Holombra?" asked Ginger, as she, also, put her feet up, getting comfortable.

"No," replied Agatha. "I opted to go visit a perfectly, lovely farm instead. The farm is managed by a supremely handsome man, the husband of my friend Idda Costa Littleless. To see the farmhouse, "fazenda" is like stepping back in time. It is built high off the ground with very thick walls. All the construction is stucco and tile. Very high ceilings, stately antique furniture made of gleaning dark woods and such a scenic quiet air inside. There is usually a breeze blowing lazily through the house. No screens on the windows, because for some amazing reason they don't have the bothersome insects like flies and gnats. They just have the most beautiful wooden shutters on the windows that open and close."

"It sounds so very, lovely," Ginger said, dreamily. "Tell me about the flowers."

"Well, this particular farm has hundreds of roses. There was a magnificent azalea blooming on the side of the house. It was close to 15' tall and twice as wide, just a mass of riotous pink blossoms. There was a tunnel of bougainvillea edging the driveway in a profusion of pinks, purples, and corals. Oranges hanging on the trees and the sweet fragrance from the blossoms on the coffee trees. Always, fresh fruit everywhere to eat. And, Ginger, the foods of Brazil are just as glorious."

"I read in a cookbook that there are three great cuisines in the world. The French, the Chinese and the Brazilian. I think it has to be the way the foods are prepared, instead of the ingredients used. Often, succulent flavors are sealed into foods by first sautéing them in onions, tomatoes, peppers, garlic, and herbs, etc. The Brazilian dishes are famous for their many subtle, tantalizing flavors. The food was delightfully delicious!"

"How was your Portuguese?" Ginger wonders. "Did you have any problems?"

"Well, the most extraordinary things happened to me in the grocery store," chuckled Agatha, remembering out loud.

"There is a coffee bar as you walk into the store that serves free coffee. Now, mind you, their version of coffee is an entirely different concept from an American version. To describe it accurately to you, Ginger, it is like chewing on a coffee bean that is smothered in three cups of Karo syrup. Very strong indeed. Well, to continue, there I was, standing and chatting to my friend Idda, who at that moment had her head turned and was talking to someone else. I slid her demitasse cup closer to mine, thinking I was making more room for others when it dawned on me that I had taken another ladies coffee. She was looking at me in the most surprised way, and hesitantly and timidly telling me in Portuguese that that was her coffee. Of course, I apologized in English which didn't make a bit of sense to her."

Ginger was laughing so hard her sides hurt.

"That isn't all I did in that store," confessed Agatha with more chuckling. "I was paying for my groceries and feeling quite pleased with myself for noticing a darling, little girl standing behind me. She was staring at me like I was a peculiar species in the zoo. I, graciously, gave her a copper penny thinking she might like it. I then picked up two bags of groceries and started walking out the door. Something made me look over my shoulder and there was the cashier, the bag boy, the little girl, and the girl's mother all flapping their arms around and making sounds at me. Yes. I had picked up their two bags of groceries and in their minds the exchange was a penny! I did not go back to that store for fear that they would put me behind bars as a thief. My stay in Brazil would have been much longer."

"Then," continued Agatha, "there was my hostess. She knew I needed quiet to sleep. The neighbor's dog would make the most awful racket at night. So out of desperation, after calling her neighbor repeatedly, and asking her to please, silence the dog, my hostess took matters into her own hands. She is a dentist and has medications at her fingertips, so she decided to medicate this noisy little dog and make it sleep. I told my hostess that I was decidedly nervous about that idea and here in the U.S. you could easily be sued for everything you own. She thought the matter over and decided to call her neighbor one more time. The neighbor informed her, *No, indeed. Do not medicate my dog. I will hold it in my arms all night in my bed to keep it quiet,* she said."

"Oh Agatha!" laughed Ginger, "Did you get any sleep?"

"I slept like a log," replied Agatha. "And I fell in love. I fell in love with not only the country of Brazil, but also the Brazilian people. They really are the friendliest, warmest, most giving people I have ever met. Someday I hope to return. After I have learned a little more Portuguese."

Bulbs need room to flourish

When bulbs become overcrowded, the flowers start to diminish in size. Such was the case of Irene Stout's garden. She had huge clumps of daffodils, but no blossoms. Feeling quite discouraged she picked up the telephone to call her friend, Agatha Chrysanthemum.

"Agatha, do my daffodils need fertilizer?" asked Irene. "They don't bloom anymore. They are just leaves."

"No, Irene, they don't need fertilizer, they are overcrowded. When you have clusters of bulbs that produce a lot of flowerless foliage, they need to be dug up, divided and replanted separately at the right spacing."

"When is a good time to dig them up and divide them?" Irene asked.

"It's best to leave them undisturbed until the foliage dies back."

"I have noticed the flowers on the daffodils have been becoming smaller each year." Exasperated, Irene went on, "I guess that is what was happening. They were starting to choke and needed more space."

"That's right, Irene," responded Agatha as she took a fortifying sip of coffee. "Here is a little of what I know about daffodils. Are you ready?"

"Fire away, Agatha! That's why I called!"

"Daffodil is simply the English version for narcissus, whether the trumpet is long or short. Narcissus is a large genus consisting of many hundreds of varieties and species that flower from late winter through spring. The genus is divided into various divisions. Division one is the commonly known daffodil. The daffodil bulb is what is known as a True bulb. A True bulb has a paper-like covering or tunic that protects the scales from drying and from mechanical injury. Many plants such as daffodils form new bulbs around the original bulb. These bulbs called offsets, develop from buds within the base of the mother bulb, and produce new plants. When the bulbs become overcrowded that is when it is time to dig them up and transplant them.

"A little secret, Irene, to help your bulbs along when you transplant them is to put phosphorus below where the bulbs will be located. Remember, below the bulbs. That's important. A general 'rule of thumb' when transplanting is to plant them 2 – 3 times as deep as the bulb is wide."

"That's great, Agatha. Thank you so much. Do you know the poem by William Wordsworth?" A relieved Irene asked. "It goes like this:

"I wandered lonely as a cloud
That floats on high o'er vales and hills,
When all at once I saw a crowd,
A host of golden daffodils.
Beside the lake, beneath the trees,
Fluttering and dancing in the breeze."

"Yes," smiled Agatha. "I knew a special man, Warner K. Buchanan, that enjoyed quoting that by heart. He loved daffodils. And they are an especially beautiful flower."

"…And then my heart with pleasure fills
And dances with the daffodils."

Childhood memories surface in a daydream

The sun was warm on Agatha's face as she sat down in her Boston rocker. She noticed a ladybug crawling on her windowsill and felt her eyes closing, she let sleep carry her away to a land of memories.

It was music day. The children in the old, one-room school were singing a song…"Ladybug, ladybug fly away home. Your house is on fire, and your children aren't home. All but one and her name is Agatha, and she hid under the frying pan."

All the children pointed at Agatha when they sang her name. She hated it.
 To remove herself from the torment, she turned her head and looked out of the schoolroom window. On the windowsill was a baby robin. It had just hatched. The baby, still wet from its safe, quiet home inside the shell, fell over and died.

Her dream then shifted (as dreams do) back to a conversation with Dr. Summers on the topic of ladybugs.

"Why are we having such an influx of ladybugs?" Dr. Summers asked her in a cross voice. "Are they harmful?"

"When it comes to insects," replied Agatha, "there are good guys and bad guys. Ladybeetles are good guys. They are even beneficial to us. They eat aphids, scale insects, mealy bugs, mites and insect eggs. The Asian ladybeetle came here from Southeast Asia, China, in the early 1900's. In China, they overwintered in the cracks of cliffs, ledges of stone, etc. Here in the Midwest, we don't have many cliffs, so they crawl into the siding of our homes, cracks of concrete, anywhere they can. They try to come into our homes to stay warm."

"They are a nuisance and have a nasty odor if handled which tends to discourage some predators from eating them. As far as we humans are concerned, they will do no damage and can be picked up with a vacuum cleaner or can just be ignored. They are not migrating more than a mile or two in an area, and they will most likely not get worse. In fact, they will probably become less of a nuisance as disease and parasites bring them under control. They are annoying and inconvenient because they are so prolific, but they are harmless. The coleopteran: Coccinellidae, Lady Beetle, is one of our more important naturally occurring predators."

Then Agatha's dream jumped back to the little girl looking out the schoolroom window at the baby robin. Dr. Summers was in the dream at this point rather than the teacher.

Little-girl Agatha turned her tear-stained face to Dr. Summers and with eyes brimming over with tears asked, "Why, Dr. Summers? Why did the beautiful little robin have to die?"

Dr. Summers answered her. "Because, Agatha, the baby robin only had half of its heart. The other half was still in heaven, so the mommy and daddy robin let it go back to heaven so it could have a whole heart. And the baby bird gets to live in heaven, too!"

Agatha awoke with a soft smile on her face.

"Ladybugs to baby robins? It must be time for my cup of tea."

Consider home's architecture when creating the landscape plan

Agatha had been invited by the "Gardeners Guild" (a dedicated group of women) to give a short introduction to landscaping. The invitation came by mail. Agatha smiled as she read the invitation as nothing had been left to chance. They had even chosen her topic.

She graciously accepted. It wouldn't have been prudent to do otherwise. Not in a town that was just a whistle-stop and where nearly everyone was on a first name basis.

The meeting was held in the home of Mrs. Flora Potts. Agatha was given a burgundy, brocade chair in the front and was surrounded by 30 interested faces of the guild. Almost all were holding little notebooks with pencils poised.

"Before a spade ever hits the soil you need a pencil and paper," Agatha told the group. "Your thoughts, ideas, colors, sizes, and textures all should be put on paper. A good landscape plan should be attractive and should complement the style of architecture of the home. Divide the property into three parts: the public area, the living area, and the service area."

"The public area is the front of the home. A simple rule is to keep the front uncluttered. The public area should be attractive all year and easy to maintain. The plants chosen should be in scale and frame the house. Car and foot traffic are of utmost importance, so driveways and walks must be functional."

"Another simple rule – focus on the front door. An example would be if the house is Colonial, hedges on either side of the front entrance would be in keeping with the Colonial style and would serve the job of leading people to the front door."

A woman raised her hand and asked, "What makes a good hedge?"

"Hicks yews are very good," Agatha answered.

"The outdoor living area should be planned as another room of the house. It can be made private with the use of wooden screens, shrubs, and trees. This is my favorite part," Agatha said, smiling. "In a true Cottage garden, both front and back doors lead you straight out of the house into the garden, so you feel that the garden is an extension, almost part of the house. It pulls you in and feels as furnished as any room in the house. This outdoor living area can have a patio, a lawn or a deck. The patio or deck does not need to be large, as long as the hard surface will seat the immediate family."

"The third area of concern is the service area: the vegetable garden, storage structures, and in the case of farmsteads, the entire courtyard with barns and other buildings. All of these should be considered. Many backyards open into unsightly alleys or include near the alley unattractive areas for collecting trash. The architectural style of the house is an essential consideration in the landscape design. Such as Colonial, Early American, Victorian, Ranch style or a Contemporary. Each of these calls for a slightly different style and approach."

"Remember this is just a tiny bit of information on the topic of landscaping. It is crucial to spend time and thought on planning the landscape around a home. Just as you would an interior room before you build or redecorate it. The garden area lives on for years and is an integral part of the home."

Dealing with a pest problem

The rosebuds were eaten and full of holes. The apple trees had lacy brown leaves. The peaches had thick clumps of beetles piled on them. The hanging clusters of green grapes were just an appetizer before eating the leaves of the soybean fields. Moreover, adding insult to injury, the beetles were flagrantly and unashamedly behaving indecently.

Agatha had had enough. She marched off to the telephone with fire in her eyes to call the U of I extension service, intending to speak to Mr. Etam Upp, the head of the nursery department. She knew when it was time for some pest management.

Mr. Upp answered on the first ring, and after exchanging pleasantries, Agatha continued, "I know that two of the guidelines for pest management for insects are the economic injury level and the aesthetic injury level. I have to tell you, Mr. Upp, that the Japanese beetle problem has exceeded and certainly justified a treatment plan when they are causing such a variety of plants and fruits such extensive damage. I also know that a delicate balance exists between predators and prey and how important it is not to upset this balance. Mr. Upp these obnoxious beetles have reached an intolerable level."

Mr. Upp answered, "That is so very true, Agatha, insects have many natural enemies:

birds, fish, amphibians, reptiles, and mammals all feed on insects. Even certain protozoa and nematodes may attack them. Disease pathogens such as bacteria and fungi. However, these methods alone are usually not effective when a severe pest problem occurs."

They both settled down for a nice comfortable chat, Mr. Upp by stretching out his legs, crossing his feet and putting them up on his desk and then inserting a toothpick in his mouth. Agatha, on her end of the telephone, sat back in her Boston rocker with a glass of iced chamomile tea to calm and soothe her indignant and intolerant outrage.

Mr. Upp delved into history as they chatted. "Insects and their relatives have been co-existing with man for thousands of years. Although many people may consider insects undesirable pests, of the approximately 850,000 identified species, it is generally agreed that "only" a small number (approximately 10,000) of these species are destructive. The remaining balance may be broadly grouped as either beneficial or harmless insects. What you are seeing Agatha, is the damage from the Japanese beetle's mouth. They feed on solid material, and their mouths have specially developed structures called mandibles that act like jaws with teeth. The damage caused by the insects can vary according to their mouthparts. They can cut and chew plant tissue. Beetles and caterpillars may completely defoliate a tree or leave behind ragged, hole filled leaves."

Flipping the toothpick to the other side of his mouth with his tongue, he continued, "This, in itself, as you know, won't kill the plant, but it does stress the plant, which weakens it for other problems to start up."

Agatha, sipping her tea, said, "I know the four steps of life stages for this type of insect: egg, larva, pupa, and adult. I know the larva can live in a different habitat from the adult."

"Absolutely right, Agatha," approved Mr. Upp. "This particular beetle emerges in mid-June through mid-August. During this time, we see the beetle and the damage it causes, then as you put it, (he chuckled), the indecent behavior happens, or we could say "mating." They then lay their eggs in the sod, which eventually turns into a white grub that wreaks havoc on our lawns. The larvae feed on grass roots. We can see the results of this damage in late summer and early fall. During the wet Spring season, we have just made the grubs very happy, so now we have an excess of beetles. This cycle will happen all over again next year. The natural control is the weather. Drought or even a dry Spring will do wonders in controlling the Japanese beetle. People can try and control the beetle with Sevin or another insecticide that has carbaryl in it and later treat their lawns for grubs with diazinon, bendiocarb, etc. with these you apply the spray or the granules to a small area then apply ½ inch of water before treating another small area. The beetle won't lay eggs in disturbed soil such as crop fields, but they absolutely adore well-maintained and manicured lawns. They love corn silk."

"I'm thoroughly fed up with this obnoxious beetle," snarled Agatha, "I'm going out to spray my roses with Sevin, snip the live beetles in half with my clippers and in September I will treat my lawn. Thank you, Etam, you have helped me plan my killer campaign. I feel much better."

To this, Etam commented, "Be sure to follow the manufacturer's instructions on all chemicals unlike my twin brother, Euripides Upp."

Direct sunlight is unhealthy for African Violets

The African violet was sitting on a southern windowsill in full sunlight. It no longer produced clusters of lavender blossoms. The leaves had turned a pale green. It looked as if it did not feel very well at all.

N. Terry Gate used all the proper fertilizers. The room was kept at the right temperature, approximately 65-75 degrees during the day and about five degrees lower at night. The soil it was precisely what the directions on the bag recommended for African violets. All in all, Terry felt as if she had gone over and above the 'call of duty' in treating her African violet with thoughtfulness. However, something was wrong. Bugs, maybe? A call to Agatha Chrysanthemum was in order.

Agatha was elbow deep in flour, with her kitchen warm and wonderful aromas colliding. A saucepan of russet potatoes boiling, buttermilk warming to room temperature and Mozart's Concerto number 3 in G…then Agatha cocked her head listening. Was that the telephone or the music? She couldn't be sure, so she picked up the phone.

"Hello?" She said getting flour all over the phone and her cheek.

"Agatha, it sounds as if you have a whole symphony in your house!" said Terry.

"Are you having a party and if so, why didn't you invite me?"

Agatha laughed, "No, Terry. I am making yeast rolls out of potato dough, and the music provides the creative atmosphere I need." She continued working while holding the phone to her ear with her shoulder.

"Oh, Agatha, I am murder on houseplants! I always read up on my plants and go precisely by the instructions, and I still manage to kill them off. In my mind, I have 'Murderer' burned onto my forehead, and I still keep trying to grow them in my house. This time it is my African violet. It is dying, and I am killing it."

"Tell me where your violet is," Agatha said as she kept on working. She listened to all that N. Terry Gate had to say. As she slid the baking sheets into the oven, she said, "Terry, I think I can help you. Let me get off my feet while these rolls bake, and I will tell you what the problem sounds like from the information you have given me."

"First of all, light is usually the most limiting factor affecting the growth of plants in an interior. Without light, green plants cannot manufacture food, soon decline, and die. In your case, it is more of a reverse effect. The light intensity is causing you problems. The full sunlight you described to me, on a southern exposure would be great for a geranium, but not an African violet. The excess light is retarding growth and must be reduced.

Try an eastern windowsill for starters. Light plays a significant part in the health of house plants. There is the intensity of the light, the duration of the light, quality of the light, which gets into supplemental lighting such as fluorescent lamps. Sunlight like you are using is the cheapest source of light and contains the full spectrum of light necessary for good plants growth."

"I have a question to ask you, Terry?" said Agatha. "Do you have any gas in your house?"

"Why, yes, I cook on a gas range. I prefer it to electric ranges."

"You may need to check it and see if there is a leak," said Agatha. "Many houseplants are especially sensitive to small quantities of escaped gas. Poor combustion in coal furnaces and kerosene heaters can be equally harmful especially after kerosene heaters are turned off. Tomato plants, African violet blossoms, or freshly cut carnations are good gas indicators. Tomato plants will droop and twist abnormally, and the leaves will turn yellow. African violet blossoms will wither and drop prematurely, and carnation flowers will "go to sleep." Proper ventilation is important for plants as well as people."

"Oh, Agatha, thank you so much. I didn't mean to interrogate you, but you are always such help. How are the potato rolls?"

Agatha struggled out of her Boston rocker and took the lovely, golden rolls out of the oven. The fragrance was heavenly.

"I like potato rolls because the yeast cells love potato starch, and usually that combination is sure to produce the lightest and the moistest rolls."

"I'll send you some of these rolls to have with your Thanksgiving dinner," said Agatha.

Disbudding mums takes courage

There was a cold nip in the air, which meant the start of another long winter. Great flocks of geese were flying over and a full Hunter's moon was predicted tomorrow night.

Agatha sat down in her Boston rocker to make a list of things that needed to be done. Raking leaves was chore number one. Putting fresh sawdust in the chicken house was a job for her young friend, Hardy Effort.

She stopped rocking and sat in quiet thought, wondering why working with her chrysanthemums always took such courage. It was a time of year to once again, approach her chrysanthemums with determination. Chrysanthemums are called hardy perennials the same as peonies, tulips, lilies, and daylilies. "I always think of my dear friend, Dahlia Holstyn when I think of my mums. Perhaps, it is because starting in May I disbud my mums, peonies, and dahlias so that the size of the flower will increase as it develops. That takes courage."

She thought of her friend Dahlia and the tremendous courage she had. Dahlia was the same age as Agatha. The difference being that Agatha could think of something and jump out of her chair and rush off to do it, but not Dahlia. Dahlia had been using a snappy, modern walker instead of giving in to the luxury of not using her muscles and sitting in a wheelchair. "That must be part of the reason that disbudding my mums reminds me of her, because she is one of the most cheerful people I know and has more courage than ten average people and because of the disbudding in her life, her flower is the biggest and most beautiful of all...her cheerfulness." Remembering, she put her mind through the steps of disbudding. Avoid removing the terminal or top bud, as all the energy will go into this flower bud resulting in a larger flower. The disbudding process continuing until August for the mums.

It was now nearly November, and it was time to look at her mums. Once again, summoning up the courage not to merely pinch the new buds off, but more drastic measures were now necessary to get them through the winter. She walked out to her garden and started cutting back the stems of the mums to within five inches of the ground. She then dug up and transplanted the mums while they were dormant, to make room for other plants. She moved the clumps to a sunny location to save for cuttings for next spring and applied a light mulch.

Now she was ready for next May when she would root some of the cuttings for another season of gorgeous chrysanthemums. She usually filled her daffodil beds with chrysanthemums in the spring once the daffodils had finished blooming. That would give her color all year.

"Disbudding and cutting back mums to five inches takes courage for a gardener," she thought. "Just like my dear friend Dahlia. It takes courage to be cheerful when she can't jump up and go. However, the cheerfulness she always shows to others is priceless. Just like the big, beautiful flower of the peony, lily, daylily, mums, and dahlias that happens when the flower is disbudded. The result is evident in color and size. It is priceless."

Eat your dandelions, don't kill them

Weeds are plants growing where they don't belong. Weeds are usually controlled in home lawns because they distract from the overall appearance of the turf. High-quality lawns normally are judged by their uniformity. So, read Agatha as her reading glasses slipped lower and lower down her nose.

She tossed the article on beautiful lawns aside and got up to fix herself a nutritious salad full of appetizing and healthy greens. Among the fresh spring greens was one of her favorites. Dandelion greens. She had read that the bitter leaves help the body digest rich foods. She thought that was a good idea since she had just eaten two cream horns accompanied by a cup of tea.

There was a knock on the door, and there stood Stella Door.

"Agatha, I am famished! What are you having for lunch?"

Agatha took her friend by the elbow and guided her into the kitchen.

"Sit down, Stella. I am just about to eat my salad of dandelion greens." She said as she put another plate on the table.

"Dandelion greens!" shrieked Stella. "Agatha, I spend a fortune every year on herbicides trying to get those horrible things out of my lawn."

"Well here is your chance, Stella to do something for your lawn. Eat them." She said with a delighted twinkle in her eyes. "And by eating them, you will be doing your body a tremendous favor."

Physicians from many centuries ago recommended eating this plant for its medicinal qualities. It is especially good for the liver, stomach, and gallbladder. Each leaf has vitamin C, which helps the immune system and heart disease. It also has high amounts of calcium and a rich concentration of vitamin A."

"I have recently read that if eaten in the spring that the roots and leaves stimulate the flow of bile, the body's fat emulsifier, in the liver and gallbladder. That is why I am fixing this lunch, Stella. I just had two pastries, which are very, very rich and these dandelion greens will help kick it out of my system. I hope."

Stella took a tentative bite of the delicious looking greens, hard-boiled eggs, onions, and beets. Chewing slowly, she got a speculative look in her eye and said, "By heavens, Agatha, I think you've got something here! This is delicious."

"I have this bare patch of ground next to my shed," Stella mused as she munched on her salad. "I could pull up some dandelions from my lawn and plant them there as a little kitchen garden. What do you think?"

"I think that is a terrific idea. Dandelion, clover and creeping Charlie are all broad-leafed weeds. People generally use chemicals such as a post-emergent herbicide, 2, 4-D, to control these weeds. A systemic herbicide. However, your idea of pulling them up is also, reasonable as long as you don't have too many of them."

"While we are on the subject of weeds, Agatha, what is that purple plant I see blooming all over?"

"That is called henbit (Lamium amplexicaule). Chickweed (Stellaria media) is also, one that you will see frequently. Both of these weeds are cool-season annuals. Early fall to mid-fall is a good time to control cool-season annual weeds, such as henbit, and cool-season perennial broadleaved weeds, such as dandelions. Control is often successful as weeds prepare for winter dormancy."

"That's it!" announced Stella as she scooted back her chair. "I am going home to plant my kitchen garden and it is going to have lots of dandelions in it!"

Evergreens and evergreen hedges

The speaker asked the question, "Do you ever prune in July?" The auditorium full of people was silent mulling over the question. It was a seminar for gardeners called The Soft Pinch.

Agatha Chrysanthemum was sitting between two of her fellow gardening friends, Ophelia Jolly and Bea Phatt. Ophelia bravely raised her hand and said, "Yes."
 The speaker whose name was Hiram Wright nodded at Ophelia and said, "That is correct if one is referring to evergreens and evergreen hedges." "Late March and early April or even early July have consistently proven most satisfactory for pruning to avoid a spring flush of growth. Mid-winter pruning often results in freeze back of the cut stub causing loss of additional branches near each cut stub. Every plant tends to look pruned after the pruning. With new growth appearing in late April, your efforts are soon concealed. Keep in mind that we are talking about arboryitae, yews, and junipers. These three are usually pruned again in early July to prevent the development of a ragged appearance. This is often called a "soft pinch" because it may be done with the fingers. Pines can satisfactorily be pruned only in late June and early July. There is a reason for not pruning late in the growing season, and that is

so you don't force new growth which can lead to winter injury."

Mr. Wright continued, "I would specifically like to mention the Yew shrub. The (Taxus) yew is a wonderful group of plants and valuable because of slow growth, wide adaptability, extreme shade tolerance, and ease of pruning. Many of you have yews planted as a foundation planting around your home, and some of you may even have a yew hedge. (Agatha was very interested in this part of the seminar as she had a yew hedge surrounding her antique rose garden.) The spreading yew and similar forms are vigorous growers and will eventually become very large plants. When yew are growing will, pruning every spring and again in mid-June is necessary to maintain shape and compactness. When severe cutting back is necessary to reduce their size, they may be cut back as much as 50% and still make a robust recovery.

"A general procedure for pruning is to cut back the current season's growth to a cluster of side branches. Make angle cuts whenever possible. These cuts may be made in late March and again in mid-June. For heavier pruning, cut back to the end of the two-year wood. Make close cuts at a crotch or among a cluster of side branches. These openings will permit sunshine to stimulate the growth of inside twigs and dormant buds."

"For severe pruning cut to 50% and that is possible, because small green twigs and dormant buds occur throughout the plant. Make angle cuts among these bud and twig clusters or close cuts at crotches. Every remaining twig or stub should have green growth or visible dormant buds. Severely prune in mid-April or late April when new growth will quickly shade the large limbs and prevent sunburn."

Agatha turned to her friend Bea and said, "I cannot imagine 'soft pinching' my whole hedge of yews surrounding my roses. My fingers would be sore and stained green for days. I think I'll stick to my hand clippers." Bea tucked her arm through Agatha's and laughed as she said, "Being what I like to refer to myself as pleasantly plump, I would prefer to let my shrubs grow naturally and forget 'pinching' them and admire my hedges and refer to them as naturalized plantings."

Ophelia had one or two yews pruned and styled to look like spirals and even one that looked like a duck. Of course, she disagreed with Bea.

Florida's tropical growth captivates winter visitors

The old school bus rumbled to life with a promising roar. Smoke came pouring out the back in not so promising puffs. It was painted a dark green and was truly, just a frame of an old bus. The roof was now a canvas canopy, and there were no windows. It was all open.

The line of people took the surging sound of the old motor in stride. They knew that it was just part of the atmosphere of their tour ride.

The location was Hummock Groves in Southern Florida. A tour was about to begin through some of the ancient, native growth of old Florida. There was the added attraction of viewing some alligators.

Agatha Chrysanthemum was all smiles under one of her many straw hats. She was filled with eager anticipation to see, smell and absorb some of the tropical growth. The air was warm and balmy with a hint of sweet fragrance that made her nose twitch with excitement.

The guide was the bus driver. He had a full gray beard and a prosperous stomach defined by red suspenders. His voice when he spoke was more of a forced wheeze, but he knew his plants. He also, knew that he had a busload of frozen northerners thawing out in the warm Florida sunshine and that most anything he said would be delightfully interesting.

Off they bumped. They rounded a tight corner and came nose-to-nose with an enormous semi-truck full of freshly picked oranges. After squeezing by this obstacle, the guide told them that Florida's second crop was sugar cane. Of course, that left fruits such as oranges and grapefruits leading. They also produced many vegetables.

The woods were full of old Ficus trees that resembled the Banyan trees of India. He told them that Ficus trees were very thirsty trees and their roots would spread for miles looking for water. In India, a Banyan tree was known to cover five miles. Agatha was slightly skeptical over that piece of information.

As they bumped along, a beautiful Ficus tree with a trunk as wide as a small playhouse caught her eye. It had a blanket of pink bougainvillea cascading from the branches to the ground. It was indescribably beautiful.

The loud screech of a bright green bird kept demanding attention. The guide pointed to a philodendron with variegated green leaves as big as dinner plates.

"This plant," he told them, "is non-parasitic. It grows up the trees but does not hurt them. It gets its own nourishment."

There was a pointed plant growing like a tall ground cover called "Mother-in-Laws Tongue."

Then the bus rumbled to a halt at an alligator pit. The attention of the busload of people was complete.

"Alligators are strictly meat-eaters," the guide wheezed in a forced voice. "They have 72 teeth, and if they lose a tooth, it will always grow back. They now live about 40 years. They used to live up to 70 years, but pollution has changed that."

Agatha enjoyed seeing the alligators, but the awe-inspiring sight of the enormous Ficus trees and philodendron were much more impressive. They made her potted Ficus tree in her living room, and the philodendron in a hanging basket in her kitchen look like the babies that in reality, they were.

Four Kinds of Ticks

Iva Gotrocks lay down on her bed for a short nap. She had been dead heading her peonies and roses all morning. That bent over at the waist position had done a number on the small of her back. Ladybird sailed up on the bed and snuggled down beside Iva.

Ladybird was a two-year-old tabby cat that went everywhere with Iva. She thought a nap was just the thing to see her through the afternoon.

Just as Iva was closing her eyes, she noticed a movement on the comforter. A place where there shouldn't have been any movement. Peering closely, she saw it was a tick. She blamed Ladybird.

Iva had just read an article on ticks. She got out of bed to find the article and settled down to read it again. "In this area, four species of ticks are commonly found on household pets. Three of these (the American dog tick, the lone star tick, and the black-legged or deer tick) are most likely to be acquired away from the household, while the fourth, the brown dog tick, has adapted to living in kennels, homes and dog houses without reverting to another environment." "The differences are quite easy to understand when you realize that the primary host of the brown dog tick is the dog, whereas the other species preferred different-sized hosts at different life stages and digest their blood meals while hidden by soil or leaf litter. In contrast, the brown dog tick frequently climbs after feeding and can be found at the tops of curtains, behind cove molding's and even in furniture. The brown dog tick does not survive cold weather as well as the other three species, at least partially because it does not cover itself in any insulative material."

"When looking for hosts, ticks frequently climb to the tops of grasses and wait for a host to come along. When motion or smell leads a tick to "think" that a host is near, it waves at least one pair of legs in the air, hoping for contact by the host it has sensed." Iva gave a shiver.

"Disease from ticks in this area are rare. The Black-Legged tick transmits Lyme disease. Rocky Mountain spotted fever is even rarer and is transmitted by the American dog tick. The lone-star tick and the black-legged tick transmit a disease called human granulocytic ehrlichiosis. These diseases are not a threat to most people and are all treatable by physicians."

"Tick removal is best done with tweezers. It is a good idea to put the tick in alcohol so that it can be identified by a professional entomologist if there is a problem."

"Mercy!" Exclaimed Iva to Ladybird. "This raises the hair on my neck! How many hundreds of times have I pulled a tick off of you cats and never had a problem?"

Both the American dog tick and the black-legged tick (deer tick) migrate to the edges of lawns. Homeowners may wish to spray or dust with one of the acaricides such as Sevin, Dursban, Diazinon, Malathion, etc."

Iva tossed the article aside and snuggled back down beside Ladybird who purred like a freight train. "Not too worried are you dear?" she asked the cat.

"I'm not either."

Gardeners keep the Latin language alive

Agatha had been invited to give a short talk to the tenth-grade science class at Wabash River High. The class had been studying botany, the study of plants. Agatha decided to talk to them about how early botanists developed a system for naming plants.

The bored class of 15-year-olds all shifted in their seats and sat up a little straighter as Agatha briskly strode into the room. This older lady piqued their attention in her woolen cardigan and sensible shoes appearing on their turf.

"Hello, class," she said with a smile, making eye contact with most of them. The class responded by giving her their full attention, as Agatha had somehow made them immediately feel as if she was genuinely interested in each one of them as an individual. A rare gift.

"How many of you know Latin?" Agatha asked.

One hand went halfway up. "Just as I thought," she said with a smile. "For something we refer to as a dead language, it is used quite often these days, especially by gardeners."

She leaned back against the teacher's desk and launched into her talk. "Early botanists were interested in developing a system for naming plants so that they could be conveniently studied, and records of the studies could be kept and compared. Carolus Linaeus, known as 'father of botany,' was an early botanist who presented in his book, Species Plantarum, published in 1753, the system that we use today for classifying and naming plants.

"Linaeus' system was based upon the sexual parts of plants, in other words, the types of flowers and the number and kinds of flower parts a given plant exhibited. He classified over 7,300 species of plants using this system. He named them using a binomial system which gives all plants and animals two names.

"The binomial system for naming plants gives each plant an official scientific name. This scientific name consists of two names: the genus (the first word and always capitalized) followed by the species (not capitalized).

"The scientific name is in Latin, which is the international language of science."

She turned to the blackboard and picked up some chalk.

"An example of the use of the Chart of Latin/Common Names: Latin nomenclature to identify on a specific individual plant."

Acer – Maple

Acer rubrum – Red maple or swamp maple

Acer rubrum 'Red Sunset' – Red Sunset Swamp Maple

A girl chewing on several strands of hair was interested in spite of herself, held up her hand.

"Yes," encouraged Agatha, as she pointed to her.

"My mother wants a 'rose of Sharon' for Christmas. Is that all I have to ask for at the store?"

"A superb example," beamed Agatha.

The girl stopped chewing on her hair and felt proud that she had asked a decent question.

"The name 'rose of Sharon' is commonly applied to two plants, one Hypericum calcinum, a foot-high groundcover that blooms in midsummer, another Hibiscus syriacus, a shrub up to 15 feet tall that blooms at summer's end – neither of them roses. By relying solely on the common name, you could easily buy one plant when you thought you were buying the other one."

Agatha walked around the classroom, all heads swiveling to follow her movements.

"Don't get me wrong," she said. "I love the common plant names such as love-in-a-puff, pigweed or pussytoes. But being able to call a plant and identify it, by its proper Latin nomenclature saves a lot of confusion."

Agatha stopped by the young girl's desk and asked her what her name was.

"My name is Barb Berry," she said with a mischievous twinkle in her eye.

"Delighted to meet you, Barb Berry. I am Agatha Chrysanthemum, and you are welcome to visit me anytime. Maybe we could dig up one of my roses of Sharon's for your mother."

Grapevines need support

A strong gusty wind was blowing. The vines of the grapes were reaching for something to twine around with each gust of wind. They looked remarkably healthy with leaves the size of dinner plates.

Goldy Muscat and Agatha Chrysanthemum were strolling around Goldy's garden when one determined vine wrapped around Agatha's neck.

"Goldy!" exclaimed Agatha. "These vines need something substantial to climb, so they don't grab, in desperation, a human walking by."

"Help me, Agatha. I need some guidance on re-doing my trellis."

"Well, Goldy, the culture of grapes for Bacchanalian purposes is outside my brief knowledge," she said with a twinkle in her eye. "But, for a home garden, there is an endless variety of sizes and designs used to support grapes. Whatever the design, use materials that permit long-time use with a minimum of repair. Wood, metal, masonry, or a combination of these is appropriate although wire mesh is not recommended. Ideally, a trellis or arbor should be constructed before spring following the first growing season. The grape planting is more or less permanent, and the support trellis should be built to last 20 or more years. The structure must, therefore, be strong enough to bear the weight of mature vines and a full crop of grapes.'

"Are my purposes bacchanalian?" queried Goldy.

Agatha gave a hearty laugh.

"No, Goldy. I think I am safe in saying they aren't Bacchus was the Greek and Roman god of wine and revelry. I think your grapes are for juices and jams."

"There are American varieties and French-American hybrids. The grapes you have growing here are Concords, which are American. The more popular system of support for Concords and other American varieties are the 4-cane Kniffin, the Umbrella Kniffin, and the High cordon systems."

"The 6-cane Kniffin system is preferred for most French hybrids."

"American grapes make excellent dual-purpose vines when trained on arbors, on a pergola for a summer roof, on a fence or wall-almost anything will work. Good varieties, properly cared for, will produce good-quality fruit as well as shade or screen for the home landscape. Sometimes, the shade provided by grape vines growing over arbors may be as important as the fruit crop."

"Something important to remember is that grapes are one of the most sensitive plants to many chemicals, particularly herbicides containing 2, 4-D in the vicinity of the grapes. Enough 2, 4-D can drift ½ to 1 mile by air to ruin your grape crop. An injury may be indicated by misshapen leaves, tendrils, and young shoots. The leaves may have saw tooth edges and may be narrow and fan shaped. The grapes may ripen unevenly or not at all. The symptoms appear 1 to 3 weeks after exposure to the fumes."

"Sounds dreadful," said Goldy in a hushed voice.

They strolled on through the garden with Goldy quietly resolving to re-do her trellis.

Goldy turned to Agatha and said, "Now I know who Bacchus is, but can you tell me where this was said? I'll give you a clue. It was a man, and it was spoken on the way to a garden. 'I am the true vine, and my Father is the husbandman.'"

Agatha smiled.

Herbs can be grown in containers

The kitchen began to fill with a savory, homemade bread aroma. The plump red tomatoes lined up lazily on the windowsill. The freshly picked sweet basil lay drying on a towel. The loose-leaf tea was cooling in a glass pitcher waiting for the mint to be dropped in and give it that extra zing.

Agatha stepped back and looked with satisfaction on the ingredients for a light, simple summer lunch. Just as she sank into the Boston rocker to give some relief to her tired feet, the doorbell chimed, and up she popped. It was her dear friend, Corie Ann Derr, with a clay pot in her hands. She had come to share a light lunch with Agatha, and they intended to fill Corie's clay pot with herbs.

As they walked to the potting shed, Corie told Agatha how happy she was to know that she could grow herbs in a container. "It will simplify it so," she told Agatha.

"Container gardening is certainly easier on the back and knees," agreed Agatha. "Many herbs can be grown successfully in a container on a patio, balcony, or terrace. Some herbs are small and tend to get lost in a landscape; growing them in containers brings them closer to the viewer. It also helps herbs that need good drainage and tend to rot in overly wet garden soils or for tender herbs that need to be overwintered indoors. Containers are easily transported and can be arranged in attractive groupings with pots of flowering plants. Herbs can also be planted with flowers or vegetables, and that creates a colorful and interesting texture in a container.

"Any container is suitable for growing herbs as long as it has a drainage hole. However, a word of caution--plants growing in containers dry out faster than plants in the ground. On a hot summer day, a container may require watering once or twice daily."

"I can stand upright to water a container," said Corie Ann with relief. "Are herbs annuals or perennials?"

Agatha was firmly pressing soil around their arrangement of rosemary in the center, basil and some white petunias for color, while Corie Ann held the plants. "Herbs are classified either as annuals, perennials, or biennials," replied Agatha. "They can also be grown as accent plants, ground covers, or massed for effect. There is so much emphasis on the usefulness of herbs that many people do not appreciate how attractive many of them are with their eye-catching flowers, foliage, and fragrances. The wonderful thing about herbs is that the majority of herbs grow well under a wide range of soil conditions. In general, herbs do better in soils of low to medium fertility; additional fertilizer applications are not needed. Soils with high fertility tend to produce lots of foliage that is low in flavor. In addition, Corie, herbs are wonderfully resistant to both pests and diseases and are often used as repellents when interplanted with vegetables. It helps to prune the blooms of the annuals, such as sweet basil, regularly to keep the plant in the business of the production of leaves."

 As they both struggled to carry the full container, Agatha told Corie, "Now you can bring this in for the winter and continue to enjoy some fresh basil and rosemary all winter long!"

"Splendid idea!" grunted Corie Ann.

"Let's go have some lunch," said Agatha in a hearty voice.

They rubbed some garlic cloves into a slice of fresh bread topped by a slice of tomato with pieces of sweet basil and just a touch of olive oil. The fresh spicy taste exploded with flavor as they savored the flavor of summer on their tongues.

Instant results

Inspiration is the main ingredient. Without it, the first snip of the clippers could not be made. Such is the lure of topiary. Imagination is an essential asset. With imagination, the process of creation is every bit as enjoyable as the finished masterpiece.
For instant results that do not require a beautiful garden in the great outdoors, there is something called portable topiary. By training fast-growing vines over simple wireframes, at any time of year, beautiful forms can be created.

Agatha was humming a Christmas Carol under her breath as she happily groomed and shaped her already existing, fanciful topiaries. She had recently given a demonstration at the local library, on growing and training topiaries.

Agatha had opened her talk by explaining how in ancient times, trees and vines were trained for useful purposes, raising crops off of the ground, saving space, and providing shade. The Romans were the first to develop the skills. Generations after generation of gardeners have used topiary, the art of shaping plants as a living sculpture, as a means of expression.

Agatha was snipping away at a miniature rosemary tree. Her favorite and one of the easiest shapes to achieve. The professional title for the style of topiary is called a standard. A standard, a poodle, or a spiral are some of the most common types. But a multitude of shapes and forms can be achieved by training fast-growing vines over a variety of wireframes. Such as a monkey, a teddy bear, a duck, a pig or any shape that can be imagined.

The most common and reliable plants are creeping fig (Ficus pumila) and English Ivy (Hedera helix). Creeping fig roots easily and rarely succumb to insects or disease and have a fine texture, nice color and are rapid growers. Both of these plants are easy to grow and do well in a range of temperatures and light levels.

There are hundreds of varieties of ivy, and different herbs provide a useful purpose in the kitchen and a pleasing scent.
A simple form to start with is a loop. Put it in a six-inch pot and plant a sprig of rosemary or ivy at the base of the hoop. As the plant grows, twist it around the wire hoop and keep it in place by tying it in place with very thin wire. To make a hoop: a number 8- or 9-gauge wire is recommended. Aluminum wire is soft, flexible and rustproof. (Wire is sized in reverse order to its thickness- the higher the gauge number, the thinner the wire). Simply cut the length of wire equal to the total of the circumference of the circle plus two times the height of the pot plus 9 inches. (An easy way to form a perfect circle is to bend it around the

pot). All that is needed for the simple design are wire cutters, pliers and a 60-inch piece of wire. From this simple design, you can move on to a heart, a rooster, etc.

Agatha's most whimsical creation was a hanging monkey, hanging by one arm from a hook in her eastern bay window. It was clothed in creeping fig and was always a conversation piece for anyone visiting her home.

It's time to transplant frost-tolerant vegetable

It was a cloudy day. A perfect day in April to transplant the broccoli, cabbage plants and cauliflower plants.

Agatha always transplanted on a cloudy day or in the evening. These are her suggestions for setting out transplants.

About an hour before transplanting, thoroughly water the plants and soil in the containers (pots, bands, flats, etc.). The roots of the plants in the flats should be blocked out with a knife to get as much soil as possible with each root. Carefully remove plants without disturbing the roots. Keep a ball of soil around the roots.

Dig a hole large enough so that the transplanted plants set slightly deeper than it grew in the container of the seedbed. If you must use tall, spindly plants, set them on an angle in a trench.

Use a starter solution to get plants off to a fast start.

Cover the roots with soil, and firm the soil tightly around the plant. Some plant-growing containers are carefully removed before transplanting. Other containers are planted "roots and all," and the roots should penetrate the container. The following vessels are disposable and should be carefully removed while transplanting clay pots, plastic pots, plastic packs and trays; fiber pots and trays; and homemade containers (egg cartons, milk cartons, etc.). Roots penetrate the following containers, and the container should be buried, roots and all, below the soil line: Jiffy-7 (pellets); Jiffy-9 (pellets); peat pots; fertile cubes and soil blocks.

Protect plants from heat, wind or cold, if necessary. Plant protectors (sometimes called "hot caps") made of paper or plastic are available to lessen trouble from frost in the spring. Homemade devices can be constructed from baskets, boxes, or jars. Do not leave the protector over the plants longer than necessary. If the weather gets warm during the day, remove the protector or open it so that the plants receive ventilation. Wire cages placed over early tomatoes serve as a framework that can be covered with plastic or heavy paper to protect against late frosts.

April 10-25 is the correct time in this part of Illinois to set out the frost-tolerant vegetables for the summer garden.

It's time to plant tender vegetables

"A perfect time to set out tender vegetables," thought Agatha Chrysanthemum as she gave the porch swing another gentle push with her toe. Shutting her eyes, she took a deep breath of spring, inhaling deeply like a connoisseur of a newly opened bottle of wine. The scent of the French lilac teased her senses along with the wonderful aroma of newly mowed grass and freshly turned soil from a newly disked field. There was also the warm, delicious fragrance of bread baking which made her jump up with a start and race to the oven in a panic to pull her bread out of the oven.

She sniffed the air in relief as she gently plopped her four loaves of bread out of their pans onto the counter. None were burned. "All that is needed now is a fresh tomato to put on a slice of bread," she thought.

April 25 – May 10 is a good time to plant snap beans, sweet corn, New Zealand spinach and tomato plants. The tomato is the most popular garden vegetable in Illinois and Indiana. For many years, tomatoes (then called love apples) were considered poisonous and were grown solely for their ornamental value. Tomatoes are easy to grow, and a few plants provide an adequate harvest for most families.

There are hundreds of varieties of tomatoes now available. They range widely in size, shape, color, plant type, disease resistance, and season maturity. Selecting the best one or two varieties can be extremely difficult.

The letters V, F and N following the name of a variety indicate that it is resistant to verticillium wilt (V) and fusarium wilt (F) or tolerant to root-knot nematodes (N).
 There are Main-Crop varieties and Special-Purpose varieties. The Maincrop varieties are the ones that are the most familiar. Such as Better Boy (VFN – hybrid, large red fruit); Big Boy (VF – hybrid, large red fruit); Beefmaster (VFN – hybrid, very large red fruit); and Delicious (very large red fruit).
 The Special-Purpose is unique and not as easy to find. Such as Salad tomatoes, Extra-large fruit, Paste tomatoes and Container-Patio varieties. There is also, a yellow or orange fruit variety and contrary to popular belief are not significantly lower in acid content than red tomatoes and are equally safe to can or process. They taste "sweeter" than red varieties because of their higher sugar content. The following mid-season to late varieties have medium-sized fruit and are suitable for pruning. Caro-Rich (orange); Golden Boy (yellow); Jubilee (yellow) and Sunray (yellow).

Agatha walked out to her recently tilled vegetable garden and eyed the empty spot where she planned to plant tomatoes.

"Yes," she mused, "It's time."
It was also, time to get some mulch. Agatha was a firm believer in mulching her garden to

help hold in the moisture, and it helped control weeding. Straw was one of her favorites, but many organic mulches are commonly used.

Kitchen gardens date back to the 16th century

May and Mary were having a polite disagreement. It had to do with the origins of the 'kitchen garden.' Mary seemed to think that the kitchen gardens were a recent fashion for people who liked to be able to open their back door and pluck a few herbs, not having walked more than three or four steps. Mary knew better. She gently insisted that kitchen gardens had been around since the sixteenth century (1580 to be exact) although the garden type had existed for centuries.

"The old medieval kitchen gardens were a convenient production of food for the whole household. They traditionally had vegetables, herbs, and fruits and were generally enclosed with a fence. The fence could be woven branches, hedges, lattice, etc.… Hedges were usually privet (thus called because it served to ensure privacy) thorn, sweet briar, and yew," said May.

May Apple and Mary Gold were sitting in green Adirondack chairs with Agatha Chrysanthemum in Agatha's backyard. The cicadas were buzzing, crickets were chirping, and although Mary and May were lazily squabbling, there was that lovely, relaxed feeling in the air that happens on August afternoons.

"Well," said Agatha, "It is nearly the time of day for the whippoorwill to start up. To get back to your subject of kitchen gardens--- aren't they wonderful!"

"I went to a seminar several years ago in Savannah, Georgia on that very subject. The young girl that gave the talk was a talented speaker and made all of us (her audience) want to rush out and start spading our soil after the talk. The title of her talk was a little weighty. It was, "The Early English Kitchen Garden." She told us how that long ago they had Physic gardens for medicinal purposes and gardens just for pleasure, too. I found it all so very interesting," said Agatha.

She continued, "Some gardeners prefer to select a specific theme for an herb garden and choose herbs accordingly. Some examples are a kitchen garden (including thyme, sage, basil, tarragon, dill); a single-color garden such as gray-green (including horehound, lavender, artemesia, and wormwood). Also, a scented garden (including mint, scented geranium, lemon balm, silver thyme, and rosemary); or a garden with different varieties of a specific herb (common sage, tricolor sage, golden sage, purple sage, clary sage, pineapple sage). The possibilities are limited only by your imagination."

"First put your ideas on paper. Once you have decided on the typed of garden, make a rough sketch or drawing on paper. This helps to visualize what the garden will look like and will help in figuring the number of plants needed. Think about the staging (shorter plants in front, taller towards the back) as well as the succession of flowering. Consider the specific requirements of the herb (sun vs. shade; moist vs. dry soil). It is so much easier having it on paper than trying to remember it."

May dreamily said, "I like the idea of a single colored garden. All white flowers, perhaps."

"I am happy with my kitchen garden, hodge-podge as it is,' said Agatha. "I have a little of everything. Lettuce, pots of perennials and many herbs. My yew hedge that surrounds it does take some upkeep, but the effect is well worth it. And I like the convenience of it, near my back door."

All three ladies sat quietly in dreamy contentment. As the sun sank lower, the first call of the whippoorwill was heard.

Knowing when to plant makes all the difference

Spring and winter kept playing tug-of-war. A few brave crocuses were popping their heads up out of the ground.

The chirping and singing of the birds was growing in volume. Thoughts were turning to gardening.

Artie Choke and Agatha Chrysanthemum were taking their early morning constitutional – brisk walk. They were discussing their vegetable gardens.

"The success of the garden depends to a great extent upon the site," huffed Agatha as she set a brisk pace, arms pumping.

Art not to be outdone started listing the following points.

"Good soil. Adequate sunlight. Away from trees and shrubs. Near a water supply. Close to your house. Suitable to the landscape design."

"Why, Art!" Agatha said with admiration. "That's it in a nutshell. The soil, good soil is essential for a successful garden. A soil that is in good "tilth," or physical condition, is loose and easy to work, and has water holding capacity, drainage, and aeration."

"Manure is a common form of organic matter used in gardens. It will also fulfill part of the fertilizer requirements of the soil.

Because manure is low in phosphorous, 1 to 1½ pounds of superphosphate should be added to each bushel of manure."

"Let's talk about when to plant," panted Art. He felt like he might choke. Keeping up with Agatha, even though she was nearly ten years older, was more difficult than he expected.

"How early can you start planting a vegetable garden?"

"It depends upon the hardiness of the vegetables and the climate of the area. Certain vegetables can withstand frost, while others cannot. Vegetables are classified as very hardy, frost tolerant, tender and warm-loving, according to their ability to withstand freezes, cold temperatures or heat."

"Very-hardy can be planted as soon as the ground can be prepared. Spinach and lettuce seeds may even be broadcast on late snows over soil prepared in the fall."

"Frost-tolerant, or semi-hardy, can be planted as early as two or three weeks before the average date of the last 32 degrees F. freeze in the spring."

"Plant tender, not cold hardy, at the average frost-free date in the spring."

"Warm-loving, or heat-hardy, require warm soil."

"When is the last frost-free date, Agatha?" gasped Artie Choke. He was starting to make a dreadful wheezing sound.

"The frost-free growing season varies greatly, depending on where you live. In the more northern areas of the State, it is about 160 days and more than 200 days in the south."

"The average date of the last 32 degrees F. freeze in the spring here is April 20. There is a 50 percent chance that a freeze will occur on that date."

Here is some help for summer gardens:

- Very-hardy vegetables – cabbage, mustard greens, onions, peas, Irish potato, spinach, and turnips – March 25-April 10
- Frost-tolerant vegetables – beets, broccoli plants, carrots, Swiss chard, lettuce head plants, parsley, and radishes – April 10-25
- Tender vegetables – snap bean, sweet corn, and tomato – April 25-May 10
- Warm-loving vegetables – lima beans, cucumber, muskmelon, pumpkin squash and watermelon – May 10-June 1

"We live on a line between the central and southernmost part of the State, so some of these dates, Art, could be earlier."

"Agatha," wheezed Art. "Let's sit down and have a coffee and donut!"

Missing tool leads to mysterious end

A soft, misty rain was falling adding to the gray color of February. Everything looked bare and cold. The branches of the old maple tree looked dead.

Melvin McMurray pulled on his waxed canvas barn coat and a sturdy pair of rubber boots. As he walked out the back door, a drop of rain fell off the edge of the porch roof. It ran down the back of his neck as he stepped down from the porch making him shiver.

He squinted up through the maple branches, and another cold chill ran down his spine. He couldn't shake off a dark foreboding that all was not well. He listened for an unusual sound, but all was quiet – a wet, heavy quiet, but for the soft drip of the rain.

Melvin was on his way to the tool shed. He made a habit of stopping work 10 minutes early to scrape and wash the earth off the gardening tools and then he would wipe them down with a slightly oily rag.

He always bought the best tools that he could afford – tools made with good steel and strong ash. He knew it was better to make do with a few high-quality ones than many second-rate tools that do not hold up well over time.

He loved his tools and kept a good stone and file in the tool shed to keep a sharp edge on the spades, hoes, and shears. Once a year he would send them to an experienced grinder to have them sharpened properly.

The most important garden weapon in his armory was his spade. He favored a long-handled spade. He had a long-handled digging fork. He had three hoes: a Dutch hoe, a swan-necked hoe and his favorite, the onion hoe. All of these well-loved tools were hanging in an orderly fashion along the east wall of the shed. Melvin picked up the oily rag and ran a practiced eye over his tools. He intended to give them a little buffing to keep them in tip-top condition for spring. There they were – the spade, the digging fork, the three hoes, the iron rake, the two trowels and the long-handled shears.

The wheelbarrow, rubber hoses, and the watering can took up the west wall. On the north wall, Melvin kept insecticides and fungicides. The pump sprayers, syringes, and jars were organized and tidy. He used some of his old soda bottles from soft drinks and even a few tin cans to store some of his chemical mixtures while he rinsed out his sprayers. Even these were arranged by brand and variety.

Melvin tried to whistle "You Are My Sunshine" to cheer himself up as he reached for his oily rag. He gave another shiver as that cold drop of rain on his neck seemed to turn his spine to ice.

His head jerked up, and he thought, "Something is not right!" Looking at the east wall of tools again, his eyes traveled across them starting in the order of the spade first and on down the line. His sharp pointed trowel was missing. There was not hanging on its nail. He had left the tool shed door open and looking through it toward his large compost heap something caught his eye. Squinting through the misty rain, he was baffled.

"Why would my trowel be lying in the compost heap?" he thought to himself.

Perplexed he tugged up the collar of his coat and walked toward his eight-foot high compost pile. Reaching down to rescue his wandering trowel, he jerked upright with a loud gasp! The blue and white fingertips of a hand were touching the tool. On closer inspection, it looked like a woman's hand.

Mystery in the garden continues

The pale, blue hand looked cold. Melvin McMurray was loath to touch it. Nevertheless, it was protruding from his compost pile, and as reluctant as he was to touch it, he knew he should feel it and see if it was warm or cold. Slowly, he hesitantly reached down and held the pale hand between his hands. It was cold.

All at once, Melvin was seized with a frantic urge to find the body that belonged to that hand. He started digging in a frenzy. Compost went flying. Just as he would make a little headway, more compost would slide down from the top.

Eventually, he had moved enough compost to find the face. He gasped and sat back on his heels. It was Mrs. Flora Potts of the Gardening Guild. He moved more compost to listen to her heart and feel the pulse in her neck. Her left hand lay on top of her chest, and her fingers were wrapped about a Coca-Cola can. At this point, Melvin ran to the house and called the ambulance. (911 was still not available.) He was shaking so hard that he had trouble pushing the buttons on the telephone. He needed someone to talk to, so he called Agatha.

"Agatha!" Melvin cried with a shaking voice. "I just uncovered Flora Potts from my compost pile, and I am quite sure she is dead."

"Have you called the police?" Agatha asked in her imperturbable, steady way.

"No," answered the agitated Melvin. "I called the ambulance, and then I called you."

"I'll call the police," said Agatha. "I know the Chief of Police, Howell I. Keeporder. Then I will come right over."

"Thank you, Agatha," said Melvin gratefully. "Why would Flora Potts be in my backyard, in the first place? I can't imagine."
 Melvin hung up the telephone and reluctantly went back outside to the compost pile with a heavy heart. That is when he noticed a one-gallon, black, plastic bucket that had rolled a foot or two from the compost pile. It was half-full of compost, and it was not his.

The compost pile was Melvin's special joy. It should more accurately be called a decomposition heap, for most compost piles are mainly made up of raw material from the garden: grass clippings, sod, leaves, cornstalks, hedge clippings, weeds and discarded plants. Kitchen scraps such as fruit and vegetable trimmings can also be added to the pile. Never put grease, fat, meat or bones as they attract rodents. Likewise, unshredded twigs and branches of trees or shrubs should not be added to a compost pile, because they take too long to decompose.

The general idea is to heap up different types of refuse, layer by layer. Alternate moist and green materials like grass clippings or kitchen wastes with dry materials such as leaves or cornstalks. Combine the dry and moist material in equal portions.

Chopping the materials into smaller pieces will significantly increase the rate of decomposition. The microbes needed for decomposition of organic matter are already present. However, adding one inch of garden soil will speed the composting process.

The pile should hold a certain amount of air and not be too squashed. It needs to be moist, not wet. Heat needs to be generated. As the material gradually decomposes, the center of the pile reaches temperatures of 150 to 170 degrees or more.

This kills some of the weed seeds, insect eggs and disease organisms that are present in raw material. The finished compost is soft, loose and smells somewhat like freshly plowed soil. The compost pile needs natural or artificial shade, not full sun. And most definitely not Flora Potts!

The police and Agatha arrived at the same time. They all stood in a row looking down at poor Flora Potts. The Chief of Police turned his penetrating, steely, blue gaze on Melvin and said, "The question is: 'Why was Mrs. Flora Potts in your backyard?'"

Mystery of the missing tool: Part III

The Chief of Police repeated his question to Melvin McMurray, "Why was Mrs. Flora Potts in your backyard?" The Chief of Police, Melvin and Agatha Chrysanthemum all stood at the edge of Melvin McMurray's compost pile looking down at the very still body of Mrs. Flora Potts, president of the Gardener's Guild. Former president of the Gardener's Guild.

Melvin pointed to the one-gallon plastic bucket near the compost pile and said in a quiet voice, "That is not my bucket."

Howell I. Keeporder pointed to the Coca-Cola can lying on Flora Pott's chest next to her hand and asked Melvin, "Is this yours?"

Melvin unhappily answered, "I'm afraid it is. It is from the North wall of my tool shed. That is where I keep my chemicals such as pesticides. I sometimes put my leftover chemicals from my sprayer in a soda can or bottle while I rinse out the sprayer when I am going to use the sprayer again the next day. I am very careful not to keep chemicals in my sprayer unless I am using my sprayer. I am starting to wonder if I have been very careless and made a grave error."

The gloomy weather did not help the grim, dismalness of the occasion. It was oppressively quiet, but for the steady drip of the rain.

Agatha said in a sorrowful voice, "I just talked with Flora on the telephone yesterday, and she told me that she was going to re-pot her Impatiens. It was one of her favorites. A New Guinea hybrid called 'Lasting Impressions.' She told me, in a tickled way, that she 'had something up her sleeve' to give it is that before the next Gardener's Guild meeting which was to be in her home. She wanted her Impatiens to be extra stunning!" Melvin looked at Agatha incredulously and asked: "Do you think Flora Potts crept over here last night, wormed her way into my toolshed for a trowel to get some compost for her Impatiens?" His voice was sliding up the scale close to soprano stage as he asked this in shock. "All she had to do was ask."

Agatha started to soothe him when Chief Keeporder interrupted her and abruptly said, "Yup! The way I figure it is that while she was in your tool shed, she got thirsty."

"Oh dear!" said Agatha. "You know Flora moved here from Atlanta, and her favorite drink was a 'Co-Cola.' That is what they call a coke in the South. Co-Cola. She also had a smelling disorder. What I mean is, she had terrible sinus trouble and lost her ability to smell."

"I remember what was in that coke can," said Melvin. "I was treating my lilacs, my peach trees and birch trees for borers. I use a chemical with the common name chlorpyrifos. One of the trade names is Dursban. I spray the lilacs and the peach trees in mid-June. Just the trunks and the limbs. I spray the birch tree, just the trunk, and limbs, in mid-May. I remember not being able to put the lid back on the Dursban so I poured it in a coke can because most spray chemicals last for three or more years. I intended to use it up over the next two weeks. I forgot."

"Oh, Melvin!" exclaimed a heartbroken Agatha.

"A crushed and grief-torn Melvin said, "I know better. It says right on all pesticide labels: '…keep pesticide in original container.'"

Chief Keeporder said, "I believe it also, says that it is a violation of Federal law to use the product in a manner inconsistent with the labeling."

"This is a lesson to me," mused Agatha. "I often read that many pest problems can be avoided by other prevention methods such as planting resistant varieties. Birch varieties such as Whitespire or Heritage river birch are less susceptible to bronze birch borer that is the common paper birch. I'm so sorry, Melvin."

Agatha continued, "I dislike using chemicals so. The labels on chemicals are very important. There are three levels used on a label of a pesticide that gives the toxicity from low to high. They are Caution, Warning, and Danger-Poison. To protect others and ourselves we must take the time to read the label. The danger of any product is evaluated not only by its toxicity but also by the degree of your exposure to the product. Deaths from occupational exposure to pesticides are very unusual. Most deaths by pesticides are children under ten years of age. Nearly all pesticide deaths are caused by eating or drinking the product. This is what happened to poor Flora Potts. Remember pesticides are not the only poisons: Plants, fungi, and bacteria produce some of the most toxic compounds known. Nature is the 'best' chemist.

"The lesson here," unctuously said the Chief of Police. "Is to never, ever put a dangerous pesticide in any container other than the original container. Accidents happen.

Most Illinois soil has been formed from material originally moved by glaciers

Agatha Chrysanthemum glided down to Sara Bellum's Lawn Equipment shop in her butter, yellow 1937 Cord 812 Supercharged Phaeton. It had red leather interior. The shop was on the East Side of town on the edge of the Embarrass River. (Pronounced Ambraw by the locals)

(A little girl asked her mother why the river was named Embarrass. The mother replied because we can see its bottom.)

Bellum's had all the many motor-driven machines that come to our aid when gardening. They plowed, hoed, sowed and mowed. Depending on how deep your pockets are and on the size of the garden you can treat yourself and try to justify the expense. Agatha pushed open the door wondering if she should invest in an old, broken down mule.

Hanging on the wall was a chart full of fascinating information. It talked about soil. "The starting point for any soil is the parent material from which it is formed. Most of the Illinois and Indiana soils have been formed from material originally moved by great sheets of glaciers. During the Ice Age these glaciers, which may have been a mile or more thick, pushed southward from Canada until they covered most of the northern United States. Although ice invaded Illinois and Indiana during several glaciations, it was the two later ones the Illinosian and the Wisconsian, which had the most, influence on our present-day soils. Thousands of years elapsed between these two glacial periods when allowed enough time for a thick highly weathered soil to be formed from the material left during the Illinoisan glacial period."

"Like giant bulldozers, the glaciers scraped and leveled the areas they touched. As they moved, they carried along large amounts of rocky material, grinding much of it into a variable mixture of gravel, sand, silt, and clay and redepositing it as 'glacial till.'

"Sometimes there were warm spells when the ice melted as fast as it moved down. If these spells were prolonged, the material carried by the glacier piled up in a low ridge or a moraine" where the end of the glacier stood. Morainal ridges are common, especially in northeastern Illinois."

"During the mild periods, enormous quantities of runoff water from the melting ice carried glacial material out into a floodplain below the moraines, where it was redeposited in layers as outwash. Large amounts of finely ground rock or 'glacial flour,' were deposited in the broad river valleys. During colder weather when the streams dried up, winds picked up some of this fine dust from the dry valley floors and deposited it on the uplands over a large part of the state. This silty, wind-blown material is known as 'loess.'

"Most of the best soils here have been developed from thick loess. In fact, about 64 percent of the Illinois soils have been formed from loess."

Native vegetation determines the kind and amount of organic matter in the soil. In this area, two types of vegetation, deciduous-hardwood forests and tall-grass prairie, have given two distinctly different classes of soils-timber soils and prairie soils. Undisturbed forest soils have a thin, moderately dark top layer of some two or four inches. Most prairie soils, however, have a dark surface layer that is fairly deep. A lovely, rich soil."

"Many soils are now acid because the calcium originally in them has been leached away. This happens through weathering (time). Soil development is more rapid in humid climates that support good growth of vegetation than in dry climates. As soils go through the more advanced stages of weathering, they slowly decline to lower and lower levels of productivity. These soil changes involve long periods of time, which run into thousands of tens of thousands of years."

"Weathering, of course, depends on climate. Rainfall, freezing, thawing, wind and sunlight are all directly or indirectly responsible for the breakdown of rocks and minerals, the release of plant nutrients and many processes affecting the development of soils."

"The best evidence seems to indicate that the climate of this area was not greatly different from 4,000 to 6,000 years ago. Present climate in this area is of the continental type with hot summers and cold winters."

After digesting all of this fascinating information, Agatha decided she felt quite young. After all, what are 70 to 80 years compared to 4,000 to 6,000!

Mulch is definitely a good thing

"Agatha, yoo-hoo, Agatha are you home? Please, Agatha, you must be home," breathlessly said the tiny, little woman as she fluttered her hands helplessly, by the front gate.

Agatha poked her head, topped with one of her famous straw hats, around the corner of her house, and said, "Mercy, Carolina! Whatever ails you?"

"Oh Agatha, thank goodness you are home. There is a big truck at my house called *CHOP 'EM and CHEW 'EM* offering to dump a load of mulched wood chips. I don't know what to say to them. Is this mulch any good?"

Agatha had come to her front gate by now. Wiping her brow and leaning against the gate, she told Carolina, "Yes, by all means, have them dump it."

Carolina Wren lived two houses down from Agatha. She asked Agatha to please, stay there, as she would be right back to talk about mulches. When she returned, she has two tall glasses of cold iced tea in her hands. The two of them sat down on the white wicker chairs on Agatha's shady front porch.

"Mulching is an excellent thing to do in both winter and summer," said Agatha. "Mulch helps keep the soil moisture and temperature levels even, thus avoiding rapid and damaging changes.

"The depth should be 2 or 3 inches of any organic mulch. Some of the best mulch materials, Carolina, are shredded hardwood bark, which is part of what you just got. Wood chips, leaves, grass clippings, cocoa hulls, straw and even sawdust, if it has been aged for one year, can all be used as a mulch."
"I thought grass clippings were a no-no," said Carolina.

"Only, if you put it on very thick when it is green and wet," replied Agatha. "People also tend to shy away from the type of wood chips you just got, Carolina, because of insects living in them or you could say it hasn't been 'treated' for insects. That is only a problem if you put it, extremely thick, up next to the foundation of your home.

"It can be an excellent place for cockroaches, which will very happily, find ways to enter your home. Wood chips in garden beds and island beds are very beneficial.

"The chips can also, be used as a durable cover for garden paths and trails through natural areas. The chips provide a dry mud-free walking surface and have a natural appearance.

"Wood chips also make an ideal groundcover for playgrounds. They provide a cushioned, non-toxic, mud-free play surface."
"How close should I put the mulch to the plant?" questioned Carolina as she took a sip of tea.

"Try to avoid burying the crowns of the plant too deeply. Doing that can lead to crown rot in some plants, and it creates a harboring place for insects and rodents. The primary purpose of mulch is to protect the root system, not the crowns.

"In addition, mulches conserve soil moisture, help maintain a uniform soil temperature, reduce weeds, and give landscape plantings such a lovely, finished appearance. I have the same mulch you just got Carolina quite thick, in my antique rose garden. It is a blessing when it comes to weeding. Mulches have saved me hours of watering and weeding.

"Remember walking in a large woods, Carolina, and how clean it is under the trees? Large trees growing in large forests naturally have a layer of decayed leaves under them. This organic layer is the home of many beneficial organisms, such as the earthworm. The leaves are also, a natural mulch."

"Well," sighed Carolina Wren, "I should get home, get out my pitchfork and get to work."

"That's the aerobic part of gardening. It keeps my hips trim and my arms firmed," said Agatha with a twinkle in her eye, knowing good and well that she wasn't so very trim or firm. "We gardeners are such a healthy bunch."

Nature creates the most beautiful gardens

The car glided to a smooth stop next to a gas pump that said Full Serve. The body lines were sleek and elegant. An example of the finest artisanship done in a grand manner. The hood and doors were silver-gray and the fenders a metallic maroon. A convertible, it's top entirely hidden from view. A lovely, large straw hat with a scarf attached that tied under the chin was all that could be seen. A lady serenely sat under the steering wheel waiting for the attendant to come to his senses. His mouth hung open, and he was frozen in a half-turn. The car was nearly 22 feet long.

"What a sweet car,' he finally said to the hat, "What is it?"

"This is a 1951 Daimler," replied Agatha as she looked up and smiled from under her hat.

"Sounds British."

"It is. I have just been for a drive in the country, and I am wondering why we go to so much trouble to landscape, cultivate, groom, and devote so much time and labor to creating gardens when nature does it all so easily and naturally."

"Why, I couldn't agree with you more ma'am. I have this here hill on my driveway, and nothing will grow. Every time I plant grass seed, a big rain will come and wash it away and leave deep gullies and trenches. The sun bakes it until it looks like a miniature Sahara Desert."

Agatha read his nametag, "Phil," but felt uncomfortable calling him by his first name, "Well, Mr…" she questioned.

"The name is Rupp," he said, "Phil R. Rupp. I have just seen the most beautiful, natural roadside planting. It was mainly daylilies and Queen Anne's Lace. There was even some bright, blue chicory blooming. Daylily is the common name. The botanical name is Hemerocallis hybrida, and that is derived from the Greek meaning 'beautiful for a day.' That is only true of the individual flower as new buds on the stalk open daily. It has thick green foliage that remains attractive all through the growing season. The daylily is a wonderful perennial that can provide colorful blooms from early spring until frost. It is sometimes referred to as a groundcover and best of all; I think it would thrive on your hillside, Mr. Rupp. The daylily can thrive on neglect and flourish anywhere. It also doesn't seem to mind poor soil."

"There are many varieties. Tall, medium and dwarf. They grow best in a medium, heavy loamy soil. However, as I said, they can thrive in poor soil. As far as fertilizing, only sparingly, if at all. In addition, an excess of nitrogen can be harmful. Daylilies benefit from high levels of phosphorous and potassium."

"Queen Anne's lace would be an attractive complement to the daylilies. Once they become established and help hold the soil in place to keep the erosion down you could plant some spring flowering bulbs such as tulips and narcissus. The foliage of the daylily would not interfere during the blooming period of the spring bulbs."

"Why ma'am, thank you. I can picture it, and I do like the pretty orange daylilies I see in certain places along the highway. I think you have just solved my erosion problem."
"By the way, ma'am, what kind of power have you got under the hood?"

Without batting an eye, Agatha answered, "The Daimler is powered by a 5.4 liter, straight-eight engine. And, if you are referring to me, it is strictly 6 a.m. caffeine."

Newly planted shrubs take a little more time and care

Virginia Cowslip had a problem. She had been given the task of watering Ann Emone's shrubs through the summer months. Ann Emone had planted eight shrubs, four different varieties, on June 6 and by Aug. 6, it was doubtful if they were all going to pull through. Virginia felt dreadful. She was 13 years old. In desperation, she telephoned Agatha Chrysanthemum.

"Well, Virginia," said Agatha after answering her phone. "My best guess, without seeing them, is that they didn't get enough water."

"I watered them twice a week and counted to 25 on each plant," wailed Virginia. "Just like Mrs. Emone told me to. Plus, we have had several inches of rain!"

Agatha thought the matter through until she came to a conclusion.

"Virginia, get ready to go. I'll pick you up in 45 minutes. My Allard hasn't been out and about for some time. We will take it for a little spin and check out these shrubs."

Agatha didn't invest her money in stocks and bonds. She collected and restored old cars and kept them in mint condition.

The car was low and red and looked like it belonged on a racetrack. The only upholstery was the twin bucket seats. It had no bumpers and a tiny windscreen. Equipped with a big American V-8 engine, Allards had cleaned up the sports car races until the Mercedes 300 SL coupes came along.

There was no ear-shattering roar or screeching of tires as she pulled out of her driveway. She eased the car onto the road as quietly and smoothly as if she were driving in a funeral procession.

Agatha, wearing a lovely straw hat, pulled up in front of Virginia's house. Virginia stared, and her heart began to pound.

"What do you call it?"

"A J2X Allard," Agatha answered.

"It looks old."

"It was built in England in 1952, at least 34 years before you were born, dear."
 Virginia slipped into the Spartan cockpit; her legs stretched out nearly parallel to the ground. "Wow!" was all she could say.

They serenely pulled up in front of a white Cape Cod style home. The questionable shrubs were lined up on either side of the front door--a foundation planting.
 Agatha kept a trowel, clippers, and gloves in all of her cars just for this kind of emergency.

She got on her knees, pulled the mulch away from four of the shrubs, and dug down about 8-inches. The soil was faintly moist with a significant amount of white chat gravel mixed in it.

"Look, Virginia, always put the plant back at the same level or depth at which it was grown in the nursery. These are container-grown shrubs. Always, remove the container no matter what it is made of. Cut the circling roots and pull the roots out straight.

"You can see that the crowns of these plants are above the soil line and the roots are still tight in the original ball. Moreover, most importantly, always, always get the air pockets out. Firm the soil, but if it is wet, do not compact it until all of the air or pour space is eliminated.

"Backfill with 'slurry.' 'Slurry' is made simply by adding soil and water as thick as soup. Fill the pit with 'slurry,' then allow time for the water to soak out to eliminate air pockets and provide good contact between the plant ball and the soil.

"Always form a water-holding dam around each plant so the water will enter the planting pit and the plant ball and not run off. Be sure to level this ring out before winter. If water stands too long and freezes (Zone 5) it can damage the base of the trunk.

"There are two types of evergreen shrubs here, Virginia, and the fact that there is so much chat in the soil has probably raised the pH and evergreens like a more acidic soil. So, aluminum sulfate and/or peat moss may be added to make it less alkaline and more acidic.

"Although we have had rain, newly planted shrubs take a little more time and care, especially with the heat wave we have just had in July. That is when a plant will suffer, and I am almost certain that there are air pockets under these shrubs.

"Time will always tell," she quoted.

When they got back in the Allard, Virginia told Agatha "thank you," and that she felt better knowing it wasn't all her fault. The Allard purred in agreement.

Nut tree attractive feature for lawn

The Black Walnut tree caught the last low golden rays as the sun sank in the west. Agatha noticed how perfectly it was framed in her window.

She turned to her friend, Phil, and said, "Do you ever think of all the people that work inside an office all day and seldom see the sun and sky? I think one window in an office should be mandatory for people to keep their sanity!"

Phil found it hard to think dismal thoughts with the spicy, aroma of Agatha's baking nut bread filling the air.

"Tell me," he said while enjoying the view of the Black Walnut tree, "How easy is it to grow nut trees in this part of the country?"

"The Black Walnut is a native species to Illinois, and it is the most dependable nut plant for this area. There are several varieties, which have superior nuts, more disease resistance, and more dependable production than other types of black walnuts. These are Sparrow, Beck, Oakes, Hare, Vandersloot and Emma K. All varieties are usually pollinated by native trees.

"Walnuts prefer deep, fertile, moist soils such as are found in river bottoms, but they will grow in a wide range of soils," Agatha continued. "Avoid excessively wet soils.

"Nut growing in this area is very possible. The Hickory species are tall, handsome trees. Many are native to this area, and some species have better nut quality while some hickories are best known for their spectacular fall coloring. Pecans are related to the Hickories, and they develop into large, attractively shaped trees, but here, you need a northern hardy pecan. There are also the Chinese Chestnut, Hican (hybrids from a hickory-pecan cross), Persian Walnut, Filbert (Hazelnut), Hardy Almond and Butternuts, which do poorly.

"The most important factors that determine whether nut trees will grow and bear satisfactorily are climate and effective pollination.

"I don't mind telling you, Phil, that squirrels and birds are my biggest problem. They are a greater deterrent to success than diseases and insects."

The sun had set, and the view from the window was gone.

"I think it is time for me to take my nut bread out of the oven," said Agatha as she struggled out of her Boston rocker.

"It smells divine," said Phil as he sniffed the air. "Tell me what is in it."

"Eggs, butter, 2 quarts of black walnuts, graham cracker crumbs, coconut and brown sugar," responded Agatha. "It is a favorite recipe of mine that I make before the Christmas holidays. I usually, freeze several loves."

"Well, I think I will plant some nut trees," said Phil as he got up to leave. "It's the perfect time of year to plant them."

"Plant several," encouraged Agatha as she wrapped a loaf of bread in brown paper for her good friend, Phil Berts, to take home.

Ornamental grasses offer unique landscaping options

Mina Pinion was bogging down in a quagmire of indecision. She was looking out the window, vacillating between planting the bare spot in the corner of her garden and the longing to start planning Thanksgiving dinner which was only 18 days away.

Mina used the ornamental grasses for shrubs, groundcovers, and screens. Many of them formed clumps that made them ideal borders, hedges, and specimens. She loved landscaping with ornamental grasses. They were low maintenance and such a showy specimen with their dramatic flower heads. And she had an impressive collection.

The bare spot in Mina's garden was begging to be taken care of, and she had decided that that particular spot was perfect for a tall striped Eulalia grass technically referred to as Miscanthus. 'Variegatus.' A three-colored striped grass (yellow, white, and green) that would grow to 6-feet tall. A very, hardy perennial grass.

She telephoned Agatha Chrysanthemum to ask her opinion.

"Well, Mina," Agatha said as she answered the telephone, "If you want my opinion, I will tell you this."

And she continued.

"The two most popular ornamental kinds of grass are the Miscanthus Sacchariflorus (Eulalia Grass) and Pennisetum Alopecuroides (Fountain Grass). The fountain grasses are the favorite.

"Purple fountain is the most popular, but it is an annual. Therefore, it needs to be seeded or carried over winter in a greenhouse and propagated each year. Many types of grasses do not make much of a visual impact in the winter. A few, however, like Pampas grass and Erect Plumed Tussock grass, carry their seed heads through the winter and can be very spectacular.

"The grass you are hoping to plant, Striped Eulalia grass, is a hardy perennial grass and does remain much of the winter. It is hardy throughout Zone 4. Five outstanding varieties of Miscanthus are excellent in the landscape. The one you chose is very striking, Mina.

"Pampas grass is the best known of all ornamental grasses. Divisions best establish it. In the northern part of its range, it is sometimes frozen out if not protected. Planted in good, well-drained soil and a protected site, it should be no problem. These plants must be propagated by divisions.

"Early fall planting is probably best for all of the divided hardy grasses, so they have enough time to root down and provide a good plant by the next growing season. Plant less hardy or more difficult to establish grass like pampas in early spring and use large, well-rooted plants. Biennial grasses will have to be planted in the fall. Seed propagation of most of the ornamental grasses should be done in a cold frame or a greenhouse much the same as would be done for bedding plants."

"Thank you very much, Agatha," said Mina. "I do value your opinion so much."

Agatha quietly smiled on her end of the telephone, as she knew very well that Mina Pinion was most decidedly of an independent mindset.

Perennial's and shrub's together in a Garden

"Using perennials and shrubs together in a garden is a good idea. First of all, woody shrubs maintain a constant presence in winter to provide interest such as stem color, fruit color, and it gives some vertical shape to the bed when the perennials go dormant."

Agatha Chrysanthemum slowly rocked in her Boston rocker, reading. It was early on a May morning. The sun had yet to put in an appearance. Agatha absently reached for her coffee and looked out the window facing east towards a sky that was filling with color, just before the sun peeked over the horizon.

"Maybe that is what I need in that bare spot in my garden," she thought to herself. She picked up the book and continued reading.

"Woody plants provide a stable green background for the flowers and wind protection as a bonus. Winds tend to come from different directions in summer and winter. Summer winds tend to blow more from the south and west; winter winds prevail from the north."

"Some perennials including delphinium and peonies are prone to wind damage and may need staking or planting in a sheltered area away from the winds. Searing winter winds may mean a heavy layer of mulch over the grounds of your perennials to prevent drying."

"Surrounding a perennial garden or border with shrubs or evergreens not only reduces the wind problem but also provides an ideal background for viewing plants."

The sun was climbing in the East, and Agatha put down her book to go and let the chickens out. She let them "free range" around her lawn during the day, but every night at sunset they would file into the chicken house, and she would shut the door later in the evening. She was very fond of her Cochin bantams and they, in return, produced an astounding amount of eggs. She had no trouble keeping protein in her diet.

Returning to the house, she picked up the book to finish the part on woody shrubs. Her mind was forming a plan to incorporate some woody shrubs in her perennial garden.

"Evergreen yews for winter greenery and maybe, a forsythia or two for spring color. Perhaps a mock orange for fragrance."
She continued reading.

"In the Midwest, you need to use the flowers of many types of plants to have flowers all season and some structure in the garden in winter. Woody plants add a great deal in the way of flowers and structure throughout the year."

Pitching old seed packets is a wise gardening move

The kitchen drawer was full of old seed packets. It was a catchall drawer and was a hodge-podge assortment of rubber bands, film canisters, nearly empty aspirin bottles and many seed packets that had been tossed in because Agatha couldn't bring herself to throw them away.

Agatha was fumbling through the drawer looking for scissors that had the audacity to turn up in the oddest places. Seeing the many used seed packets reminded her of a question that Vi Abell had asked her.

"How long are seed packets good for?"

Agatha had answered, "Only viable for living seed can germinate and grow into mature plants. Most seeds are viable, alive for one to three years depending on the conditions and where they have been stored.

"A seed is composed of three parts – the embryo, the food storage tissues, the endosperm and the seed covering. The amazing thing about the embryo is that no matter how tiny the seed is it has the genetic information that determines how the plant will grow.

"The number of viable seeds will depend upon a variety of factors including the plant species, environmental conditions, seed development as well as any injury to the embryo."

Vi had started laughing. "Agatha, you are giving me a botany lesson and interesting as it is, the answer to my question is one to three years?"

"Yes, Vi," Agatha said with an effort at reining herself in. "But, and this is a very important step, the environmental conditions such as temperature, light, moisture, and oxygen need to be adequate for germination to occur. Sometimes we tend to blame the lack of growth on the seeds when in reality it was our own fault. For example, letting the seeds get too dry after planting them.

"Forgive me, Vi, but I must add another little botany lesson. When a seed germinates the first thing that happens is that the seed imbibes or absorbs water causing the seed to swell. The radicle emerges from the seed and develops into the primary root. The hypocotyl also develops, emerges from the soil and eventually becomes the vegetative or leafy portion of the mature plant.

"These tiny, tender little shoots that emerge from the soil need to be protected from dogs stepping on them, chickens eating them as a delicious appetizer or a hundred other hazards that could crush them."

Agatha took another look at all her seed packets after recalling that conversation with Vi and proceeded to look at the dates on the packets, and with iron, courage threw out all the packs that were over a year old. She determined to plant the others as soon as possible.

She never did find that contrary and elusive pair of scissors.

Proper preparation extends the life of cut flowers

Things were hopping at the Cut N' Snip beauty salon. Ginger Wild and Hazel Witch were the two most sought-after beauticians in town. Partially, the customers were awestruck by Ginger's ability to talk nonstop. She could carry on a conversation over the roar of a blow dryer just as easily as she could whisper in a baby's ear.

The customers had learned to step over the two cats as they came in the door and to push them off the chairs if space was needed. Gordito and Zoro, the cats, never seemed to mind. But this morning was like no other. Things were in an uproar.
 Ginger finally lost her temper as she cut her finger on scissors. She unexpectedly pounded her fist on the counter and yelled. She looked around for the cats, but they had fled. Her anger wasn't directed at them, but a cat can't be too careful.

Her customer looked at Ginger in startled amazement relieved that the pounding hadn't been her shoulders. Just as things reached an astounding crescendo in walked a florist with a bouquet of fresh cut flowers wrapped in green paper. They were for Ginger.

"Oh, aren't they beautiful," cooed Hazel. "But, Ginger you know you will kill them. A flower can't last a day around you."

"True," agreed Ginger. "I have this uncanny ability almost instantly to kill any flower at any given time."

"Please, call Agatha Chrysanthemum," begged Hazel. "They are far too beautiful to last only for a day."

Ginger saw the wisdom in this, and with great alacrity, she picked up the phone and started to dial. But stopped when she heard a voice say, "Here I am girls! Under the hair dryer!"

In all of the commotion, they had forgotten that Agatha was there getting her monthly trim.

"Hand me a piece of paper. I will list some helpful points as I sit here drying."

She labeled the top of the paper PROLONGING THE LIFE OF CUT FLOWERS AND FOLIAGE.

1. Cutting stems under warm water and immediately placing them into a container of warm water prevents air bubbles from getting into the cut end of the stem, plugging up the conducting cells, and preventing or slowing down water uptake. Warm water forces out any bubbles that by chance get into the end of the stem.

2. Bacteria attack and destroy the end of the cut stem and plug up the conducting tissues. This condition is the most frequent cause for short flower life. All plant tissues in water

will rot, but leaves do so more readily. Use a bacterial (such as Clorox) or a floral preservative to control bacteria.

3. A sharp knife used to make a clean diagonal cut does minimal damage to the stem end. The only practical way to cut a flower stem with a knife is diagonal. Sharp scissors can be used when a knife is difficult to use but to avoid crushing the stem.

4. Use care not to bruise, cut, or damage the bark surface, or to break the stem when handling flowers.

5. If the water becomes cloudy, change it. Wash the container thoroughly and recut the stems to get rid of the bacteria and to expose a fresh stem end.

6. Use only clean, thoroughly washed or sterilized vases and containers.

Ginger followed those instructions and the flowers survived an incredible 14 days, looking fresh and lovely.

Proper pruning can help the tree overcome some of its damage

The trees along the town streets sighed and writhed against the intruder. The wind, relentless in its determination to bend the trees and make them bow, wreaked havoc on the small town. Its triumph was evident by the broken limbs and damaged trees that littered the streets.

Wind and ice storms often damage trees. The damaged limbs should be promptly removed, and the cuts treated to prevent insect and disease problems. Proper pruning can help the tree overcome some of the damage.

Severe topping or dehorning is often done. This practice is destructive to the tree, unattractive to the eye, and will shorten the trees' life. Topping or dehorning should be strongly discouraged.

A significant objective of pruning trees is to develop a strong framework. A storm-damaged tree must be pruned carefully to restore the health and beauty of the tree. All cuts are made at the function of a new branch when correcting damage from storms. These cuts will shed water and prevent rot while the wounds heal.

Hugo Pine was walking around his property with Agatha Chrysanthemum in tow. Some heavy-duty road construction had been going on for some time next to his property, and he was concerned that this construction was going to affect his trees.

"You are right to be concerned, Hugo," said Agatha. "Anytime we do work under a trees' drip line or cut by the roots damage to the tree can be expected."

"Soil compaction occurs more often than is realized. Operating heavy equipment or vehicles over the root systems of trees over a period of years will damage or kill trees. When the soil is wet after a heavy rain or irrigation, it compacts very easily and smothers the roots."
 Hugo walked to where a backhoe had cut a large trench. Pointing to the ditch, he asked Agatha, "Will cutting some of the roots off here hurt my Maple?"

"The fact that a back-hoe cut the roots cleanly is a big plus," responded Agatha encouragingly. "Cleanly cut roots will heal well, and new roots will develop. The fill used should be as porous as possible to permit natural drainage of water and air. When the roots of a tree have been pruned, a portion of the top of the tree should be removed, also. This is done to maintain the root-to-shoot ration. Do not cut off or pollard the top part of the tree! Select branches should be removed to the main trunk. I would call a tree specialist or an arborist to do this job."

They strolled back to the house and Agatha continued explaining. "In most cases, injury and death occur more rapidly from cut and fill damage than from compaction, but the symptoms are almost identical."

"The first symptoms are usually just a slight wilting and shedding of some leaves at the time of construction. In later years, leaf dwarfing, the dying of twigs and in the case of conifers, the excessive dropping of needles occurs. Trees damaged by construction appear abnormal in many other ways, most noticeably by dropping leaves early in the fall compared with trees of the same species in other locations."

"If the tree has been only slightly damaged, growth is slowed, and resistance to insects and diseases are weakened. Borers and aphids, both of which can damage trees, often move into construction damaged or stressed trees."

"Many diseases are soil-borne and quite destructive, especially in compacted or filled soil where the water drainage pattern has been changed."

Agatha took Hugo's arm and said, "Diagnosing compaction or smothering damage can be difficult because it takes time for symptoms to appear. Trees sometimes die five to seven years after the injury. However, Hugo, in your case, I hope for the best."

"Time will tell."

Pumpkins are not just for pies

Agatha glided the car to a halt in front of a roadside market full of an assortment of jumbled pumpkins. She was driving one of her classic automobiles from her collection. It was a deep, mossy green Lagoonda L.G., 1938. A solidly built, traditional British fast tourer with a long stroke six-cylinder engine. A beautiful specimen of an automobile.

As the car stopped all the heads at the market swiveled to see the astonishing sight of such a car with a remarkable lady under an equally impressive straw hat. Agatha popped out with her usual agility and gave a friendly smile to the whole group. Striding over to the mountain of pumpkins, she struck up a conversation with a fellow who introduced himself as "Butter."

"Big Tom Butter, ma'am. 'Butter' for short," he grinned at Agatha as he held out a huge hand. "That's a mighty fine automobile you have."

"Thank you, Mr. Butter," smiled Agatha as she shook the enormous hand. "I collect classic automobiles and have to take turns giving them a workout!"

"Look at this huge collection of pumpkins," continued Agatha. "What will become of them now that Halloween is over?"

"Well, ma'am, I can tell you what I intend to do. I am going to cook several of them." He gestured towards an old vintage Ford pick-up truck that had a bronze license plate on it that said, 'Colonel.'

"I am going to make pies, pumpkin butter, pumpkin bread, pumpkin cookies and soup," he laughed with delight, as Agatha's eyes grew quite large. "I love to cook," he said.

"And I love pumpkins!"

"I have to admit that I cook on a humbler scale when it comes to pumpkins," Agatha said with a twinkle in her eye. "I use the flowers and dip them in a batter and fry them as a delicacy. I also, take the small immature (before the seed develops) pumpkin fruit and steam it or boil it and serve it as a buttered vegetable. I also, slice it, dip it in batter and fry it. Sometimes, I serve the immature pumpkin raw and eat it with dips for snacks."

"Did you know, Mr. Butter," Agatha continued, "That the seeds of the "naked seeded" varieties do not have seed coats, and can be roasted in the oven or sautéed for snacks?

His mouth opened to reply, but she did not give him time to answer.

"Small types of pumpkins are grown primarily for cooking and pies; the naked-seeded varieties for their seeds; the intermediate and large varieties for cooking and jack o'lanterns; and the jumbo varieties for showing at exhibits and fairs."

Mr. Butter closed his mouth, and then he started to shake. He shook all over. Then a deep laugh that started way down in his belly erupted. He slapped his thigh and then he gave Agatha a click of the heels of his shoes and snapped off a crisp salute.

"Well, ma'am, you sure bested me," he said. "How long have you been cooking?"

"Oh, it's not cooking that really interests me. It is the whole "cucurbits" family that interests me. You see, I am a gardener, and I love to cook what I grow."

She gave him a lovely smile, and before she walked away, she said, "And my name is Agatha Chrysanthemum."

Queen Anne's Lace; Also known as Wild Carrot

"The woman had been walking through the forest for a long time. Scratches from briars and brambles crisscrossed her face, neck, and arms. Her faded gingham dress was just a wisp of fabric tattered and torn. Her body gaunt, her face pinched and haggard. She paused by some Queen Ann's lace and dug it up to eat the roots. A few scattered blackberries were ripening. She picked a handful of wild chives to boil in some water for soup with some other herbs if she succeeded in starting a fire. She wouldn't get the calories her body was craving, but she figured it had some medicinal value as well as taste. She dug in rotten wood for grubs."

Agatha put down her book and tried to imagine what this part of the country would have been like 250 years ago. The woman she was reading about had been captured by the Indians and escaped to survive a 300-mile journey through the wilderness back to her home. Her only protection on the journey was the torn and faded dress on her back. Barefoot, cold and hungry, she survived by eating whatever she could.

Agatha adored Queen Anne's Lace. Despite the fact that it grows wild along most of the roads, she had dug some up to plant in her garden. She liked to use it in her flower arrangements of roses and blue salvias. The wispy, delicate white blossoms enhanced arrangement was lending a fragile touch.

The botanical name, Daucus carota, hints of the possibility of carrots. The common name, Queen Anne's Lace, is also known as Wild Carrot. The wildflower blooms in May-October and grows between 48 inches and 50 inches. The water requirements are low, and it has the obliging nature of growth in the average garden soil to barren and poor soil. It needs full sun or will adjust to a half day of sun. It is a native of Afghanistan.

Agatha had just learned something new. She pushed herself out of her Boston rocker and went outside to pull up a clump of Queen Ann's lace. She eyed the dangling, little roots and thought: "If that poor little wisp of a woman can survive 300 miles without even a Compass and eat these for sustenance, I think I better taste one."

The flavor was gutsy and spicy leaving a tingling on her tongue.

Tickled, she phoned up her friend, Bea Phatt, to tell her of her discovery.

"Agatha!" laughed Bea in delight. "I will tell you something about garlic that I bet you don't know!"

"I know that garlic is from the lily family, as are onions, shallots, leeks, and chives," responded Agatha.

"Yes, that is right," agreed Bea. "People have believed for hundreds of years that garlic has magical powers. Often, you see garlic braided together by three stalks. I can, personally, verify that if you hang this over your door (or if you are lazy, pin a garlic clove over your door!) that a werewolf will never attack you. Maybe, it's a coincidence, but I have found this to be true!"

"Oh, Bea! For heaven sakes! I thought you were going to tell me something worthwhile!" Giving an exasperated chuckle, she hung up the phone and went back to reading her book.

Roses need 'coats' and 'hats' for winter

It was just the day before that Agatha had noticed the first touches of autumn. The sumac was turning red. The goldenrod was waving in the breeze. The light and dark colors of gold from the soybean and cornfields was a vivid contrast to the blue October skies. The color of the corn was nearly transparent when the sunlight touched it from a certain angle. However, today was a different story. It was gray, and a chilly breeze from the north reminded Agatha that winter was just around the corner.

Agatha Chrysanthemum put on a well-worn jacket and went out to her rose garden to see if it was time to put warm coats on her many shrub roses. She also, took a good look at her climbing roses knowing they might not only need a coat but a straw hat, too. Agatha had asked a young boy named, Hardy Effort, to come and help her after school. She took great pleasure in teaching him the right way to do things and he, being very conscientious, made a hard effort, to learn all she taught him.

"Hello, Agatha. Here I am!" called out Hardy as he popped around the corner of the house. "What do I need to get out of the garden shed?"

"Hello, Hardy," Agatha said warmly, as she stood up with her hand holding the small of her back. "We are going to need a shovel, the wheelbarrow, some of the round wire fencing, six bales of straw and a ball of twine. We won't get it all done tonight, but we will get a good start."

As they worked together, Agatha taught Hardy the best way to do the job and the reasons why it was important to do it that way. "Roses can withstand reasonably low temperatures, but in areas where frost is severe and prolonged, they will suffer a lot of damage. Sometimes to the point of death! (Hardy involuntarily shivered at her choice of words) Fluctuating temperatures can be even more harmful than freezing temperatures. A cold icy wind can be devastating as a very hard frost. So, Hardy, I want you to learn the right way to bundle up my roses, putting them into warm coats and boots and some will even require a hat!"

Hardy was jumping up and down with short little hops trying to stay warm, and he was more than willing to get started.

"First of all, fill that wheelbarrow with fresh soil from my garden. Never get soil from near the rose bushes as you could easily damage the roots. I want you to mound up the soil around the base of each bush 8" to 10" high around the canes. Get the twine and tie the canes together to keep them from blowing around which will loosen the root system. Remember Hardy, it is important to love the roses in the winter when they are cold, shivering, and bare. They will show you how much they appreciate the attention in the spring by rewarding you with fullness, blossoms, and beauty!"

"Further protection is necessary where the temperature regularly falls below zero. That is when you need the straw and wire fencing. This fence is really an old wire cage left over from my tomatoes this summer. Put a cage around each shrub and then put the coat on the rose...by filling the cage with straw. To hold the cage in place from strong winter winds either stake it or put some soil around the base of it."

"Now the climbing roses can use a hat in the winter. Climbing roses are less cold resistant than the shrub roses, generally. So, take some straw, wrap their heads in it and then we need to get some burlap so that you can cover the straw with burlap...and that is what I refer to as a hat!"

"In the spring we will remove the soil, and our roses will thank us for the extra attention through the cold winter weather by showering us with blossoms!"

"Should I cut some of these canes back, Mrs. Chrysanthemum?" asked Hardy.

"Absolutely not," responded Agatha with heart. "Pruning on the shrub roses should be done in early spring. The exception here is the climbers and ramblers. You may take out the lax stems and the dead old canes, ideally by the end of September. A general rule in gardening is not to prune late in the growing season as it forces new growth which can lead to winter injury."

"I understand Mrs. C," smiled Hardy. I will only bundle them up for winter coats, hats, and boots."

Separating bulbs increases blossoms

There is no mistaking the Sycamores. Even before you reach the enormous old trees towering over the entrance gate, your eye is drawn up the Southern Illinois driveway in early summer by hundreds of bulbs of iris and daylilies. The daylilies are all right yellow, and the irises are all a deep purple.

Chris P. Bacon had gone 'whole hog' on his lane. Hundreds and hundreds of bulbs had been planted and as fall approached, he had the monumental task of digging and separating these bulbs.

"Agatha," said Chris over the telephone. "Do you have a few moments to talk?"

"Certainly, Mr. Bacon," answered Agatha as she struggled to set down her clippers and clay pot full of marigold deadheads. "Let me get off of my feet and grab a glass of minted iced tea. I think ever so much better when I am off my feet!"

"O.K., Mr. Bacon. I am all settled. What is it we are going to talk about?"

"Bulbs," he said. How necessary is it for me to dig up and separate my daylily and iris bulbs? You know how many I have!"

"If you have noticed a decline in your blooms Mr. Bacon, chances are that they need to be dug up and separated. This will give them more room to grow, and you will notice a dramatic increase in blossoms. In addition, once you have dug them up and are ready to transplant them put some phosphorous in the hole before planting. Phosphorous encourages root development. Keep in mind that phosphorous moves very little once applied to the soil, so it needs to be put by the roots so it will be where it is needed. If mixed in the soil where the roots will go it will be utilized by the bulb roots."

"Do the bulbs of the daylily and iris look the same?" asked Chris P. Bacon.

"No," replied Agatha. "The iris bulb is a rhizome. It grows horizontally under the surface of the soil. The iris is propagated by cutting the rhizome into sections leaving a fan of leaves with each section of root."

"The daylily has a 'fleshy root' just like a peony. Some varieties of daylilies have what might be considered a rhizome type root system. Daylilies are hardy, herbaceous plants with a perennial growth habit."

"The definition of a bulb is any plant that stores its complete life cycle in an underground storage structure."

"What is the general rule of thumb on how deep bulbs should be planted?" asked Mr. Bacon.

"The general rule is two to three times as deep as the bulb is wide."

Agatha heard a rooster crowing in the background. "How are the Bantams?"

"They are doing wonderfully, Agatha. The hens are marvelous setters, so I have an abundance of baby chicks."

"If I remember right it was your Uncle, Sir Loyne Bacon, that encouraged you to raise chickens?"

"That's correct, Agatha,' said Mr. Bacon. "He said the scratching and the pecking are good for the soil. Although, I personally feel he was tired of my two pet pigs 'Crisp' and 'Tender.'

"They are no longer with me," he sighed.

Agatha was afraid to ask where they were, so she told him goodbye and picked up her clippers to continue her deadheading. She had a smile on her face as she thought of Chris P. Bacon branching out into chickens.

"A contradiction of words," she thought.

Solving common lawn problems

Agatha Chrysanthemum woke up to her phone ringing. It was her dear friend Leopold. Leopold was frantic with distress. The problem was his lawn. He had had such high hopes of lovely, velvety expanse of green turf---thick, weed-free grass. Instead, his lawn was thin and full of a weed that stuck to his clothing and a delicate, creeping, green weed with small white star-like flowers.

Agatha told Leopold that it was not even necessary for her to see his lawn to help solve his lawn problems.

First of all, the thin stand of turf could indicate poor lawn care practices such as mowing too short, improper establishment and poor fertility. Perhaps he chose the wrong grass species for the site.

"There is a recommendation for mowing a lawn," she told him. "Mow as necessary and remove no more than ⅓ of the grass at any one mowing. A good height for cool season grasses, such as bluegrasses, ryegrasses, fescues, and bentgrasses, is 2 to 2 ½ inches."

Also, he should consider underlying soil problems. The ideal pH for turfgrass growth is 6-7. The best time to get a soil sample is when soil temperature is above 50 degrees F.

"There are three kinds of basic weeds: grasses, broadleaves, and sedges. The weed that stuck to your clothing, Leopold, is a broadleaf weed called Bedstraw or Cleavers.

The delicate little plant that creeps everywhere and is especially found in the shade of trees and shrubs and the north sides of buildings is called the common Chickweed. This is spring, and it is very normal to see them.

"You have two choices," she told him. "You can try either a mechanical or a chemical solution. If you are mechanically inclined, dear Leopold, then dig and pull them---simple and effective. But if the problem is too big for that, then you have to use a chemical.

"The best weed control is maintaining a dense, vigorous turf. In your case, Leopold, I suggest an herbicide. There are many herbicides available."

She cautioned him that when using any pesticide, read, understand and follow the label directions.

"The best time to apply herbicide is when the air temperature is between 65- and 85-degrees F. Watch the wind to avoid chemical drifting. A good time is early in the morning as the air is usually more still than later. There needs to be adequate moisture so that the weed can take the systemic herbicide and translocate it through the entire week. So water first and don't apply if rain is expected within 24 hours.

"Of course, Leopold, if your lawn is just too discouraging and in such poor condition you could completely reestablish your turf area. A drastic method that will totally eradicate your problem is to use a nonselective herbicide (e.g., glyphosate) that kills everything. Then you must correct the soil pH. Correct drainage and fertility problems and then select the correct seed or turf and give it the proper long-term care.

"The definition of a weed, Leopold, is that it is a plant in the wrong place. A healthy stand of turfgrass enhances the beauty of a landscape and should not just be taken for granted.

"I hope this troubleshooting talk solves your problem, dear Leopold. Next time, please don't call until after 6 a.m. when I have had my cup of coffee," she said.

Such a lovely basket of summer fruit

The little girl stood in front of the teacher's oak desk. She held out a beautiful red apple with both hands. It was shining like it had a coat of varnish on it having just been polished on her apron.

Amos, Agatha's little brother, was walking through the orchard swinging a basket of summer fruit. So, thinking and remembering, Agatha turned to Hardy, her yard boy and started teaching him some gardening facts as they walked towards the fruit orchard. Hardy worked for money, but he learned bushels of facts. Agatha saw to that.

"Midwinter temperatures of 0 degrees F. usually kill some fruit buds on peach and nectarine trees. All of the fruit buds on these trees may be killed when the temperature drops to -10 degrees F. Spring frosts of 30 degrees F. or below during or after bloom may kill some or all of the blossoms or young fruits on all types of fruit trees. The earlier in the spring the tree blooms, the more likely that frost damage will occur. Though individual species vary, the general order of bloom from earliest to latest is apricots, sweet cherries, peaches, nectarines, pears, sour cherries, plums, and apples."

"That is why we seldom have a bountiful apricot crop in this area, Hardy, and that is also why peach orchard producers are shaking in their boots at this time of year. Spring is a little early this season, and everything is bursting into bloom. As pretty as it is, it could cause orchard producers a few sleepless nights!"

Hardy and Agatha had arrived in the orchard, and Hardy asked Agatha, "Are we going to plant any new fruit trees this year?"

"Well, that is a good idea. Spring planting is an excellent time in all of Illinois and Indiana areas, but late fall planting is satisfactory for the southern parts of the states. The ideal time for spring planting is just after the soil thaws and before the plant growth starts. This is in March for southern Indiana and Illinois and in April for northern Illinois and Indiana."

"A basket full of healthy, unblemished fruit. In addition, to get that we need to develop a spray schedule to attack the enemies of the fruit trees. Borers, feeding insects, powdery mildew, etc.'s…"

"We are just going to address a spray schedule for apples, crabapples, pears, and quinces since they all require the same treatment."

"Before the buds swell, not later is the time to apply a plant spray oil. Spray only when the temperature will drop to freezing for 24 hours."

"When green tissue is a ½ inch out of bud and again when flower buds show color, spray with Captan plus Diazinon or a multipurpose fruit spray plus sulfur (if needed). When ¾'s of the petals have fallen, do the same treatment. A note here is that if bees are still coming to the flowers, delay the application or do not include an insecticide in the spray mix. In seven to 10 days after this repeat once more. Insecticide applications at this time and again in about two weeks are especially important to prevent codling moth larvae from entering the fruit. Continue sprays at seven to 10-day intervals until July 1. Some advice spraying at 10 - 14 days intervals until two weeks before harvest."

"It sure seems like a lot of work to produce beautiful fruit," sighed Hardy Effort. "I wonder if your brother Amos, and the Amos you talked about in the Old Testament went through this?"

Agatha smiled, "Like the phrase a 'summer afternoon' the phrase 'a basket of summer fruit' which conjures up pictures in our minds of something wonderful. Sometimes to get that 'something' wonderful, Hardy, a lot of hard work goes into it. Spraying our fruit trees keeps the blemishes off the fruit and in the end yields a healthy specimen. Such as a lovely basket of summer fruit."

Sugar Maples have great color

Agatha was gently swaying back and forth in the hammock. She was looking up through the branches weighted with lovely, dark green leaves. It was a June evening, and she had spent the day answering questions and helping her friend, Phil R. Upp, who ran the local gas station that she always frequented, choose a tree that was suitable for the spot where he wanted a large shade tree.

She thought back to their conversation from that afternoon.

"When choosing a tree, remember that the foliage of the tree has both an ornamental and a functional role. The first decision to make when selecting a tree for its foliage is whether a deciduous or evergreen tree is desired. A deciduous tree is a tree that loses its leaves at the end of each growing season. Evergreen trees maintain green foliage throughout the year; however, they do lose their foliage but not all at once. Many deciduous trees provide an outstanding show of fall color before they lose their leaves. A wide range of colors can be found depending upon the species."

"Agatha," said Phil R. Upp, "I remember a tree in our front yard when I was a boy. It had the most glorious yellow and orange color in the fall. I think it was a Maple, but I don't know what kind of Maple. That is what I would like to plant."

"There are many Maples," Agatha started quoting, "There are Norway Maples, Red Maples, Silver Maples, Sugar Maples and all of these will reach a height of over 50 feet. The Hedge Maple is a medium size tree and grows between 25 to 50 feet. The Amur Maple, Paperback Maple and Japanese Maple are considered small trees and will grow less than 25 feet tall."

"Site tolerance should be considered when planting. How large will the tree get? Is the soil wet? Is it dry? For instance, a Red Maple (Acer rubrum) likes acidic soil. It will also tolerate a wet site. A Hedge Maple (Acer campestre) and a Norway Maple (Acer platanoides) will tolerate drier conditions. Often raised mounds or hilly areas will be dried by the wind thus making it important to plant trees that will survive under dry conditions."

"What I really want, Agatha is that brilliant yellow and orange color in the fall on a large shade tree."

"I think we can narrow that down, Phil, to a Norway Maple or a Sugar Maple (Acer saccharum). The Sugar Maple as it can turn from yellow to orange to red. It is one of the most popular trees for fall color. The Ginkgo (Ginko Biloba) is another example of a large tree with outstanding fall color."

This is where Phil surprised Agatha when he turned to her and asked, "Do you know that poem by Joyce Kilmer about trees?" He started quoting it:

"I think that I shall never see
A poem lovely as a tree.
A tree whose hungry mouth is prest
Against the earth's sweet flowing breast;
A tree that looks at God all day,
And lifts her leafy arms to pray;
A tree that may in Summer wear
A nest of robins in her hair,
Upon whose bosom snow has lain;
Who intimately lives with rain.
Poems are made by fools like me,
But only God can make a tree."

"That's beautiful, Phil and I do know that one. I had to memorize it when I was a child."

Agatha smiled as she recalled the afternoon and kept on swaying in the hammock while enjoying looking at the leaves overhead from the tree that "Looks at God all day."

Tips on 'desiccating' (preserve by drying) herbs

Agatha was typing a letter on her computer and becoming increasingly proficient on the keyboard. Her main use of the computer was to send emails to her friends.

The phone rang; causing her to jump and hit the Control button instead of the Shift button and all sorts of peculiar things started happening on the screen.

"Criminey?" She muttered in exasperation as she reached for the phone.

"Hello?" She said brightly trying to disguise the frustration in her voice.

"Agatha, is that you? Your voice sounds different."

"Hello, Rosemary," Agatha answered recognizing the voice. "How are you?"

"I need your help, Agatha. I would like to dry some herbs, and I want to speed up the process by using either my oven or the microwave. I do not know the temperature setting or the amount of time. I also, keep reading the word desiccate, and I don't know what it means. I know that masticate means "to chew." What, in heaven's name, is desiccate? I am almost, afraid to use it in case it is a bad word!"

"Desiccate?" Agatha smiled. "Means to preserve by drying. A desiccant is a silica gel used to absorb moisture. You are perfectly safe using that word, especially in connection with drying herbs."

"Well, I just picked some basil and would like to use it this winter in my spaghetti sauces and also, to give zest to my pea soup!"
 "First of all," Agatha said as she pushed her chair away from the computer so that she would not have to look at the mess on the screen. "It is important to pick the herbs at the right time of day. Gather them early in the morning, just after the dew has evaporated and before the sun is hot. This is also, a very pleasant time to be in the garden so the task can be an enjoyable one."

"I did," responded Rosemary. "I washed them under cold running water and then dried them thoroughly on paper towels."

"Very good," said Agatha with approval. "The easiest way to dry herbs is to allow the leaves or entire stem to dry at room temperature. Place them into a brown paper bag with the stems hanging out of the open end. Hang the bag in a dark, warm place (70 to 80 degrees). That takes approximately 2-4 weeks. There is another method too, called Silica sand drying."

I also, know a woman who copies the 'freeze dry' method in food stores. She uses fresh chives, both onion and garlic flavored, chops them finely, mixes them with a little water and freezes them in ice cube trays to be used when needed."

"How clever," responded Rosemary with interest.

"Now here is what you do to dry with heat. I am going to use that new word Rosemary," Agatha said with a twinkle in her eye. "If the herbs are desiccated too quickly at too high a temperature much of the flavor, oils, and color of the herbs will be lost. To oven dry, place the leaves or stems on a cookie sheet or shallow pan and warm at no more than 180 degrees for three to four hours with the door open. To dry your herbs in a microwave oven, place the clean stems or leaves on a paper plate or towel and set the control to high for one to three minutes. Turn the stems over or mix the leaves every 30 seconds. Remember to store them in airtight containers."

"Thank you, so very much, Agatha,' said Rosemary. "I will have you over this winter for a savory, basil spaghetti dinner.'

"I'll be there,' responded Agatha with a smile. "I can almost taste it!"

Tips on pruning deciduous shrubs

The forsythia shrubs were in full bloom. Masses of vibrant yellow dotted the countryside. The grass was coming alive with its fresh, bright green color. The sky was robin's egg blue. The colors of spring.

Agatha Chrysanthemum and Magnolia Star were strolling arm-in-arm through a large cemetery. They had just planted a forsythia (Forsythia spp) shrub on their friend, Dora Sclosed, grave.

"Tell me about pruning deciduous shrubs, Agatha," said Magnolia as she took a deep breath of the crisp air. "Where and how?"

"Well, dear, that depends on the shrub in question. Forsythia is a fast growing, erect and arching shrub. It is very reliable and has good foliage. It does best if pruned in late spring after flowering. I use the renewal method."

"For renewal pruning, remove a number of the old stems each year to promote new growth, maintain a moderate size and encourage flowering and fruiting. In the spring, cut out the largest stems at the crown to stimulate new growth from the crown and remaining stems."

"Sometimes when initiating renewal pruning on large or old plants, the immediate results may be unattractive. For example, I have an enormous old lilac (Syringa vulgaris), and I took out all of the old wood to the ground to remove the bore and scale damaged limbs. This also allows more air movement and sunlight, which deters mildew. Lilacs are very susceptible to scale, borers and mildew."

"Do you prune a Mockorange (Philadelphus spp.) the same way?" asked Magnolia as she learned more heavily on Agatha's arm.

"I'll tell you several well-known common shrubs that can be pruned in this manner. All of these plants flower on one-year wood: Deutzia (Deutzia x lemoinei), Kerria (Kerria japonica), Mockorame (Philadelphus spp), Wiegela (Wigelia spp.), Forsythia (Forsythia spp.), Arrowwood viburnum (Vibrunum dentatum), St. Johnswort (Hypericum spp.), and Lilac (Syringia spp.)."

"A more severe method of pruning is called rejuvenation. Rejuvenation is the complete cutting of all stems down to four to six-inch stubs. This procedure is used when multistem plants become too large with too many stems to justify saving any one and two-year growth."

"A plant that responds well to this treatment is Anthony Waters spirea. The best time for rejuvenation is February or March. Large old shrubs should not be rejuvenated in late spring or summer."

"Some important factors to remember when pruning flowering shrubs: 1. In most cases, prune after flowering. 2. Understand the plant's growth habits, such as mature size, flowering time and on which year's growth the flowers form. 3. Disease and insect susceptibility of a plant will determine what type of pruning and in some cases when it should be done. 4. Start pruning when the plant is young and form a strong frame in single-stem plants."

The two ladies had arrived back at one of Agatha's beautiful antique automobiles. A 1937 butter yellow Cord convertible. They tied on their large brimmed straw hats, sank into the red leather, and motored off to the Lanternlight restaurant to have a cup of coffee.

Turnip's sweet and earthy taste add unique flavor to hearty stew

The winter had been unusually mild. Looking out of the window Agatha could see the pale winter sun rising across the garden melting the frost. Colors were more muted, but the striking stems of the ruby chard caught her eye. She was pleasantly surprised to see that it was still alive.

Agatha enjoyed growing chard (also known as Swiss chard) because it was usually not available in the grocery store. She prepared the leaf blades like spinach and cooked the midribs or stalks in the same manner as asparagus. She also planted it as an attractive ornamental.

Chard is a member of the beet family and can be grown as a vegetable green in all parts of Illinois and Indiana. It yields well with few production problems, and it tolerates frost.

Agatha loved this time of day when the rooster started to crow. This part of the day always held a promise of good things to look forward to. Today her dear friend Rudy Bagga was coming for lunch.

Taking out a large shallow pot, she put 8 cups of water on to boil. She was going to make Kitty Murphy's Brunswick Stew. Enough for 16 servings. It was always a comfort to have some stew in the freezer for emergencies.

The next step always took a fair amount of courage, but it had to be done. So, with quiet determination and a few misgivings, she put on her coat and marched out to the hen house. The chickens were still roosting.

After dispatching three hens to the stew pot, she went down to the basement and picked out six large white turnips. Most people expect potatoes to turn up in stew, so as a rule, turnips in stew are not as common.

The hens were simmering peacefully in chicken stock. After one hour, Agatha took them out to cool and then removed the skin and bones trying to keep them in as large of pieces as possible.

Returning the meat to the chicken broth, she added ½ pound cooked bacon, six chopped onions, six garlic cloves, six large ripe tomatoes, six rotund turnips, six cups fresh lima beans, eight ears of corn, three tablespoons of Worcestershire sauce and six tablespoons of butter. This delightful concoction can cook for one hour.

Rudy and Agatha sat down for lunch. Rudy took a bite of stew. She looked at Agatha and asked, "What kind of potato is this?"

Agatha laughed and replied with great enjoyment, "That is a turnip!"

"A turnip!" exclaimed Rudy. "I seldom eat turnips."

Agatha patted her mouth with her napkin and said, "Let me give you the skinny on the turnip. They are a root vegetable, and each raw 3 ½ ounce portion contains 27 calories and ⅓ of the RDA for vitamin C.

"They taste sweet and earthy but have an unfortunate tendency to produce flatulence in humans. The British used to use them to make Jack-o'-lanterns until squashed by the pumpkin.

"Its relatives are cauliflower, broccoli and Brussel sprouts, but the turnip is known to be particularly close to its cousin, the rutabaga. Getting peeled and jumping into a big pot of hearty stew is something it particularly loves."
 Rudy had forgotten to eat and was understandably dumbfounded by all of this interesting information.

Unwatered lawns become dormant and brown during hot, dry periods

Agatha was amazed that her telephone was capable of interpreting the electrical impulses that were being fired like a machine gun gone out of control. She held the phone away from her ear and looked at it with confounded admiration. "Perhaps I have time to get a quick glass of tea," she thought. "I doubt he would notice!"

"Agatha! Agatha!" Tap, tap, tap went the phone. "Are you there?"

"I'm right here, Buff," she answered slightly out of breath, as she took a fortifying sip of iced tea.

"What, I ask you! What is a fellow to do? I refuse to spend my entire summer sitting on a lawn mower, smelling like gas, and sweating like a pig! I feel like a victim of my domain, rather than the 'King of all I Survey!'"

"First of all, Buff Alowed, are you watering your lawn regularly?"

"Not lately," he responded slightly nonplused. "We have had so much rain that I haven't needed to, however, before that I watered 1 to 1 ½ inches of water per week just as you told me. Right?"

"That's what the books say, Buff. For cool-season lawn grasses used in the Midwest like Bluegrasses, Ryegrasses, Fescues, and Bentgrasses that is the proper amount of water per week during the growing season to maintain green and active growth."

She paused. "There is an alternative. That's to let the lawn go dormant during hot, dry weather by not watering it. Unwatered lawns of cool season species normally become dormant and brown during hot, dry periods and then recover acceptably when growing conditions improve in the late summer or early autumn. During most years, lawns in this part of the country can safely survive periods without summer irrigation." "I am going to list some effective lawn watering practices."

1. Do not begin watering at the first sign of warm weather. Root-system elongation is the initial turf-grass response to droughty conditions. Do not delay watering, however, until the lawn has gone dormant. After an initial droughty period, begin watering to maintain green color and active growth.
2. To determine when to water, walk on your lawn to see if your footprints are visible behind you. On lawns in need of water, the grasses will not spring back. Where moisture is adequate, grasses will spring back.
3. Select a sprinkler based on yard size and shape.
4. Supply a uniform amount of water to the entire lawn. When sprinkling, monitor water distribution by placing coffee cans or some other straight-sided

vessels at various points beneath the sprinkler's pattern. Measure the quantity of water captured and overlap sprinkler patterns to supply the entire lawn with a uniform amount of water.

5. It is best to water deeply and infrequently. Water to the depth of the turf root system. Usually, 1 inch is adequate to supply this amount. Do not water again until the soil has dried.
6. Avoid light, frequent watering unless just seeded.
7. Water early in the day. This can reduce water loss due to evaporation and reduce the incidence of lawn disease.

"Something to watch out for when you do find yourself compelled to mow, Buff, do not mow too short. During spring and autumn, here most lawns should be 2 to 2 ½ inches high. This should be raised by ½ inch during summer. Mow frequently and never remove more than one-third of the grass blade at any one mowing."

"I think I will stop watering my lawn when we hit some dry weather and let my lawn go dormant."

"Thank you, Agatha, I don't feel like I am going to go completely around the edge now."

Agatha smiles. "You don't sound so frazzled and buffaloed now. Remember you are in charge of your lawn. Not the other way around."

She took the phone from her ear and thought it felt relieved to have a rest.

Wage war on slugs by offering them beer

Arthur Pod loathed most insects. He was a semi-avid gardener and could be seen most mornings, very early in the morning, puttering around in his garden. One of his favorite mottoes was "Early to bed, early to rise, work like heck and fertilize!"

It was a little late in the year now for fertilizing, but he had been spotted lately doing a most peculiar thing. Repeatedly, he would bend over low to the ground, straighten up, shake his head and mumble in a most dissatisfied fashion and eventually make his way around to the back of his house going through this same peculiar process over and over.

It usually had the same ending. He would abruptly straighten up, snatch his hat off his head, and throw it on the ground and thunder, "By George! Don't that beat all!"

Then, the strangest thing of all, he would go into his house and come out with several bottles of beer. He then walked slowly around his garden and for all casual purposes, it looked as if he would bend over and pour a little beer out of the bottle onto the ground. He would do this all through his garden. It was starting to be whispered around town that good old Arthur Pod's mind was beginning to head South--a sad situation.

Arthur's 24-pound cat, Whopper, usually lazily accompanied him around the garden, sharpening his claws on the fence, stretching out, watching with one blinking eye. But lately Whopper couldn't climb up the fence, and he preferred to sleep, a sleep that was more comatose than normal.

 But Arthur Pod knew precisely what he was doing. He had had a pleasant conversation with Agatha Chrysanthemum, and she had provided him with some very satisfying information. It was information that would launch into eternity one of his most repugnant enemies--slugs, shell-less snails that delight in shady, damp areas.

He had begun noticing, last summer, that an unseen and uninvited diner was making lace leaves of his hosta, violets, impatiens, and other bedding plants. These unsightly, slimy creatures also, feed on mulches, dead leaves, and other dead plant material. Agatha told Arthur that he could control slugs with baits and an interesting bait was...beer.

Ideally, the beer should have been open for six days (she hadn't given him a clue as to why), and he should place the beer in shallow dishes. Jar tops make a perfect shallow dish.
 In the morning, Agatha had told him that he should find them filled with drowned slugs and that he should empty, and refill as often as needed. The slugs are attracted to the smell of beer. They drown either because they are quite drunk or because they can't swim. Either way, it should kick them into the beyond!

However, something very odd was happening to Arthur Pod. He was finding the jar lids empty, and no slugs drowned, drunk, or otherwise.

All at once it clicked. Whopper! No wonder he couldn't climb the fence. He was soaked to the gills and listing to starboard. He would have to keep Whopper out of the garden so he could recommence waging his battle on the slugs.

Wet soil can damage fruit trees

Idelle Chattre was thinking about the time of death. Why did it happen? When did it happen? Moreover, of course, what killed the dead ones? She needed to talk to somebody.

Driving down her driveway, she avoided looking at all the dead ones.

Idelle parked her car in front of Agatha's home and made her way to the front door, stumbling over the steps as she was keeping her eyes wide open so that the tears wouldn't spill over. Everything had kind of a magnified underwater look to it.

Agatha pulled Idelle into the warmth of her home and gave her a big hug. They talked pleasantries for a moment, and then Agatha put a stop to it by saying, "Let's stop this idle chatter and tell me what the problem is."

"Why do fruit trees die?" sadly asked Idelle through her tears. "I have lined my driveway on both sides with apple and pear trees, and suddenly at least half of them are dead. They looked so pretty last spring, lining the drive, with a deep creek on either side of them full of rushing sparkling water. "They were just full of blossoms. They looked so healthy."

"The fact that they were so near water makes me suspicious," gently replied Agatha. "Wet soils are a major cause of fruit tree loss in this area because most of our soils are heavy with an excellent moisture-holding capacity. The soils here have poor internal water drainage and tend to stay wet during rainy periods in the fall winter and spring. The damage may not become apparent for six months or more after it occurs. Damage occurs to the roots and the below ground portion of the trunk. The inner-bark of these parts will be brown instead of the normal light-yellow color."

"I knew that fruit trees do not like "wet feet," said Idelle. "I thought they were far enough away from the creeks.'

"They could be far enough away from the water, but it could be the combination and proximity of the soil and the water," said Agatha. "Mind you I can only make guesses unless I can see them."

"The cause of death for most fruit trees is damage to the trunk, the crown (that area around the ground level and just below), or the roots. Injury to these parts can be caused by wet soil, winter cold, spring and fall freezes, mice, rabbits (young trees only), crown and root diseases, drought, and borers. Frequently, a combination of two or more of these is the cause of death."

"Sour cherries, peaches, and nectarines are especially sensitive to damage from wet soils. Pears, apricots, and plums are somewhat more tolerant."

Agatha put on the tea kettle to help comfort, Idelle. Agatha was a firm believer in a cup of something hot giving comfort in times of stress. In this case, she felt it would help ease Idelle into accepting the tragedy of the dead ones.

Agatha handed Idelle a steamy, hot cup of apple cider and said, "Idelle, Spring will come, and I will help you find the perfect spot for your fruit trees. We will choose it together."

They both sat in silence for a moment wrapping their hands around the cups of cider and breathing in the delicious fragrance. They were ready for a long and interesting idle chat.

What is an antique (old-fashioned) rose?

The Jekyll Tea Shop began serving tea at 2:30 in the afternoon. It was in a tiny, little town that was not on the way or convenient to anything. However, it was well worth the effort to drive there and while away a delightful hour or two.

That is just what Flora Bunda and Agatha Chrysanthemum intended to do. Flora had invited Agatha to go out for tea and asked if she would mind driving.

"Splendid, Flora! I have wanted to take out the Packard. It looks like a lovely day for a drive with the top down!"

Agatha had an absorbing interest in collecting and restoring classic automobiles. These were her investments. This particular car was a 1930 Packard '734'. There were only 150 of these made and could reach 100 mph with turbine-like smoothness. It was resplendent in a deep two-tone russet and orange. Large whitewall tires with a spare on the left front fender.

The two ladies motored down the country road at a sedate speed.

"Agatha?" questioned Flora turning to face her as she draped her arm across the back of the sea. "Could you explain the different rose varieties to me, please? I know you have some 'Antique Roses' and I know that most roses you buy in the grocery store and at the florist are Hybrid Teas. What exactly is an 'Antique Rose'?"

"Defining an 'Antique Rose' (also known as Old Fashioned) is a little difficult. The American Rose Society classes as 'old' any rose introduced before 1867, but most people are more lenient and consider anything over 75 years in age, old. The signs of an old rose are the undiluted rose perfume, superior shrubs, and more muted, pastels in coloring. Old roses are tough. They not only have charm and beauty, but they have survived on old homesteads and cemeteries, sometimes for centuries without care."

"The majority of roses come from Europe and the Orient. A few are native to the U.S. Long ago, some roses were cross-pollinated in nature, and in gardens to give us new varieties."

"In the late 1700's and 1800's, European botanists explored the world, searching for new plants. The roses of their homelands bloomed only once a year, usually in late Spring, but in China and other parts of the far east, they found roses that bloomed year-round. The plant explorers named these roses 'China' and 'Tea' Roses and brought them back to the West. They were crossed with their European cousins, the once blooming Gallicas, Musks, Centifolias, and Damasks. These crosses produced many new classes of garden roses: the Noisettes, Bourbons, Portlands, Hybrid Perpetuals, Polyanthas, and

Grandifloras. By the turn of the century, one class took over. The Hybrid Teas."

"I used to use the description of Hybrid Teas, Grandifloras and Floribundas as being the most popular roses. And then I became interested in Old Fashioned Roses and added that to my list."

"A simple classification is to use three basic groups. Species, Old Garden Roses and Modern Garden Roses."

"I can handle that last description," responded Flora. The rest gets a little complicated."

They parked on a deeply shaded side street lined with majestic old, maple trees. Agatha made a careful inspection of the Packard and decided it was safe to leave the top down.

"Flora, after all that talking I think I could drink a pot of tea all by myself!"

Green Fables

Winterberry is a good choice for a hedge

Dee Terman was making the most of her time on an unusually cold February day. Spring was just around the corner, and Dee knew that this was the time of year to plan her gardening for the next ten months.

Dee would spend hours surrounded by well-known, beautiful gardening magazines that helped to chase the gloom of winter away and made growing any plant you could think of simplicity itself! Fired with imagination, she would write a list of all the plants she wanted and then go back after a dose of reality and shorten her list by about 70 percent. February was the month she usually ordered roses, flowering shrubs and summer bulbs. It was also the month that she tried to get her fruit trees trimmed.

This year she wanted to plant a hedge between a green expanse of lawn that abruptly ended at a cornfield. To Dee, this part of her garden always looked bare and exposed.

She telephoned Agatha Chrysanthemum.

"Agatha, could you tell me a good, inexpensive hedge to plant? I don't care if it is evergreen or deciduous. What I do care about is the cost. It has to be reasonable."

"I have just the thing," responded Agatha heartily. "I was just reading an article in a newspaper about the decline of bluebirds in North America due to the loss of one of their favorite foods. A shrub called Winterbury (Ilex verticillata). A horticultural specialist says that this is due to overbrowsing by the growing population of deer. The article says that Winterbury used to cover hundreds of acres even up in Canada, but deer have decimated this shrub."

"It is a native shrub that will grow in sun or light shade. It doesn't mind if the soil is light or heavy. The wonderful feature of this shrub is that it has a tremendous abundance of bright red berries all through the winter. Since you don't require an evergreen hedge Dee, this shrub would be ideal. It is deciduous and loses its leaves in the fall, but the berries are prolific and provide a vibrant red color all through the winter."

"Oh, Agatha, I like the idea of planting a shrub that is native to the area," said Dee. "Somehow it seems right. I especially like a shrub that will attract bluebirds."

"The bluebirds do need food during the winter," responded Agatha. "They do not migrate south in the winter. Winterberry is a good choice for a hedge, but it can also be planted by itself. I am going to suggest a few more deciduous plants that would make a good formal hedge. Privet (Ligustrum spp.), Bush honeysuckle (Loniccra spp.), Spirea (Spirea spp.), Pearlbush (Exochorda grandiflora), and Buchthorn (Rhamnus spp.). All of these will make excellent hedges as long as they are pruned properly. We will leave the pruning discussion for another afternoon, Dee. I think you have enough information for now."

Wisteria, clematis both climbing beauties

Violet Able and Idelle Chattre were having a vociferous disagreement as they sipped their coffee at the Lanternlight restaurant.

Vi had a darling old outhouse that she would like to soften and help blend into the landscape. Something to quiet the look of precisely what it was instead of shouting it out to the world.

Vi wanted to plant wisteria. A very, vigorous, noble and hardy climber. She informed Idelle with a knowing look that brooked no argument. "It will grow in any reasonable soil, in fact, Idelle; it will grow in downright poor soil. In addition, it doesn't need "tender, loving care." You can hack the darn thing back as hard as you like in the winter."

"Furthermore, Idelle," she said tapping her nail on the table in a fashion that Idelle found very disturbing. "My outhouse faces south, and that is what wisteria loves best. Hates the north side. If I plant wisteria, I will have sumptuous lilac blossoms cascading like a waterfall. It is the King of climbers," she finished triumphantly.

Idelle looked pointedly at Vi's nail tapping finger and replied with dignity, "Well, Vi Able, if wisteria is the King of climbers let me tell you about the Queen!" Idelle leaned back in her chair, and Vi slid her hand off the table and quietly held it in her lap.

"Clematis does demand little special treatment, and neglect makes her appear a bit more familiar, like a chorus girl rather than the diva she is. If taken care of properly clematis should blossom from her toes to her head, but too often she appears to have a mop on top and a spindly body.

"Clematis likes a rich soil that is light and loamy. If the soil is very acidic add some lime or even mortar rubble. Clematis loves to have their feet in the cool shade, but their flowers in the sunshine or at least full light without obstructions overhead like wisteria," she said nodding at Vi.

"I have seen wisteria growing like a ceiling, covering the woods under the tops of the trees in South Carolina. The remarkable thing about clematis is that it will grow up a vine-like wisteria, pyracantha, cotoneaster, etc. using it as a host, and likes to have shade provided for the feet.

"I have been told that wrong pruning ruins many clematises. All new plants should be boldly cut down to within 9 inches of the ground. In May of each year pick out the tips of all new shoots to encourage branching. I cut back my clematis thigh-high every February of March. I have 'Gipsy Queen' and 'Pearl d'Azur.' I water liberally, and I mulch with manures, leaves and sometimes fertilize."

The two ladies eyed each other in silence. Idelle broke the quiet and said, "I think you have a viable idea with the wisteria. It is very hardy and will grow happily without much care. However, clematis is so very lovely. How about this; plant the wisteria, let it start growing and then plant the clematis and it will twine up the wisteria vine providing a sturdy host and perhaps King wisteria could be counted on to shade the Queen's feet! The only problem I foresee is the soil differences."

Vi smiled, "Idelle, I think you have solved it. I love it. And it is not only viable, but it is also absolutely smashing."

They put some money on the table and walked out of the Lanternlight arm in arm.

Author information:

Anne Buchanan James is part farmer and a whole lot gardener. Many years ago, she owned and operated Annes Perennials after completing a landscape design course in England while in college. Dabbling in topiaries while living in South Carolina, and growing old-fashioned roses to sell to nurseries, she also raised three children. Back on the family farm in Illinois, she raised grass-fed cattle in a rotational grazing program with the University of Illinois Extension Service, where she also completed the Master Gardening program. Moving to Florida, she became a park ranger for the Department of Environmental Protection. She completed a Florida Master Naturalist course with the University of Florida Extension service as well.

Part-time jobs as beach mouse researcher with Florida Fish & Wildlife, zip-line guide, and certified Wildland Firefighter gave way to working for a zoo in Tennessee. Animals and plants.

A perfect fit.

Green Fables